Riding the Waves

Finding joy and fulfilment in school leadership

By James Hilton

Foreword by Mary Myatt

BLOOMSBURY EDUCATION

LONDON OXFORD NEW YORK NEW DELHI SYDNEY

BLOOMSBURY EDUCATION
Bloomsbury Publishing Plc
50 Bedford Square, London, WC1B 3DP, UK

BLOOMSBURY, BLOOMSBURY EDUCATION and the Diana logo are trademarks of
Bloomsbury Publishing Plc

First published in Great Britain 2020

A catalogue record for this book is available from the British Library

ISBN: PB: 978-1-4729-6799-2; ePDF: 978-1-4729-6798-5; ePub: 978-1-4729-6797-8

2 4 6 8 10 9 7 5 3 1 (paperback)

Typeset by Newgen KnowledgeWorks Pvt. Ltd., Chennai, India
Printed and bound by CPI Group (UK) Ltd, Croydon, CR0 4YY

To find out more about our authors and books visit www.bloomsbury.com
and sign up for our newsletters

This book is for my Mum. She knew I was writing it but sadly did not get to see it completed. Always encouraging, she was, and is, much loved and greatly missed.

Contents

Acknowledgements

This book would not have been possible without the kindness, generosity and wisdom of the following people:

Richard Gerver, Mary Myatt, Wendy Rose, and Jann and Tony Tucker.

I would also like to thank the following people for allowing me to include their thoughts and words within the book:

Peter Anderton, Angela Browne, Clare Erasmus, Lisa Lea-Weston, Jonny Mitchell, Patrick Ottley-O'Connor, Ritesh Patel, Rae Snape and Hannah Wilson.

I would like to thank my fantastic editor, Hannah Marston, for all her patience, wisdom and advice, as well as all the team at Bloomsbury.

Foreword

No one in education has it easy and the role of a school leader can be particularly lonely. In James's searingly honest and self-deprecating account of the highs and lows of his leadership in a number of schools, we realise that we are not alone. That's why it's important to reach out, to make connections and to realise that, whatever you are going through, it's likely that someone has been through the same or similar. And these connections should be in real life, whether talking to someone or, in this case, reading a book.

In *Riding the Waves*, James takes us through the stormy and calm waters of leadership. From headship in two schools, the second one of the largest in the country, he knows what it is like to grow a school both physically and culturally and to experience the downsides. In *Riding the Waves*, he paints an honest picture from which we can all draw comfort. He shows how it is possible to talk about successes, without being boastful, and he shares with the reader, with humour and insight, the things that went wrong, even though it is clear that these didn't feel humorous or insightful at the time.

James began his career in education before there was a national curriculum, before schools managed their own budgets and before inspection: another world. And as a result, he has a perspective that provides many amusing insights comparing the old days with today's demands. It was neither all good nor all bad then, and the same applies today. Some of it, though, was both dire and hilarious.

One of the most important things to realise is that leaders do not need to be experts in everything. But they do need to make sure that they draw people around them who can fill those gaps. In James's case, this is his lack of confidence in budgets. Not that this seems to have held him back in expanding his school from a small village primary to over 800 pupils ten years later and working with the local authority to achieve this. There are insights here on how to make sure that mix is sufficiently diverse to make sure that the whole of the leadership team is greater than the sum of its parts.

This book will provide helpful accounts of school leadership together with the headlines from leadership thinkers. It walks us through the potential pitfalls, so that, for example, we don't find that we have lost the 'dressing room'; it is important to take stock of the things that have gone well, because clocking these will provide the psychological space to tackle improvements. James also provides helpful points of reflection on our strengths and weaknesses.

Then there are useful reminders for making sure that we are able to do our best work. And this means the importance of self-care, of taking time out, of having a laugh. It's so much easier said than done, but James offers some great advice for making this a reality. And this comes from a deep space, as he has the scars to show what happens when we don't: incessant mental activity leads to burn out, in James's case literally. He has observed that there are many leaders out there who are fantastic at taking care of their students and staff, selfless in their service of their communities. What some of them are not so good at, however, is taking care of themselves. Perhaps they feel that they don't have the time or that self-care is somehow, well, selfish? It could not be further from the truth.

While everyone's experiences are unique, what is powerful about this uplifting book is that we can draw universal themes from individual stories.

Mary Myatt

Mary Myatt is an education adviser and writer.
Her latest book is Curriculum: Gallimaufry to Coherence.

Introduction: Setting sail

Hello, and welcome to this, my third book on leadership and wellbeing. (Blimey – I would never have thought five years ago that I would have written *one* book, let alone *three*!) For those of you who have read either of my other two books, *Leading from the Edge* and *Ten Traits of Resilience*, a warm welcome back; you are clearly a glutton for punishment. No, but seriously, I truly value your support and interest in my work. If you have not read either of my other books, do not worry; you don't need to have done, although I *would* encourage you to buy them. (Well I would, wouldn't I?)

For those who don't know me, let me introduce myself. My name is James Hilton (sadly not the James Hilton who wrote *Lost Horizon* and *Goodbye Mr Chips* – he is always destined to outrank me on Amazon). I spent over a quarter of a century in teaching. I was in senior leadership roles for 23 years, a deputy head for eight years and a headteacher for 15 years (two schools; not at the same time!). Latterly, I was head of one of the largest and fastest-growing primary schools in the UK, with over 800 on roll. A hugely rewarding job, but not without its challenges. In 2006–2007 I had a nervous breakdown and was off work for six months. Few people expected me to return, but with medication and therapy I returned to the job and community I loved, more self-aware, a little wiser and armed with a range of coping strategies. After six more successful years for the most part, I decided to tell my story, in the hope that it might inspire others and help them to avoid some of the pitfalls that I fell into.

These days I work as a speaker and author on the subjects of wellbeing, resilience and stress management. I have a great job because I get to work with businesses and universities as well as NHS and local government staff. However, I still feel most at home with a school audience. So, I feel privileged to spend a little time together with you while you navigate your way through this book.

If you are looking for an academic study of leadership or a technical manual on how to be a leader, this is not the book for you (sorry, I hope you have not purchased this volume!). Such books have great value, but this is not what I write about. I don't pretend to have had school leadership taped; far from it. Think of it more as an exploration of a hugely important theme: how to find and maintain a sense of joy and fulfilment in school leadership even when the prevailing winds are blowing against you.

I came across this picture recently. It's a school photograph of me aged seven. Although it was taken 40 years ago (alright, nearly 50!), I do remember it being taken very clearly. This is surprising, as for the most part I can barely remember what I did yesterday. The reason that it has stuck with me for so long is because, despite my charming, if gappy, smile, the photographer humiliated me! He has probably long since shuffled off this mortal coil but, if he is still with us, I would like to think that he would be ashamed of the emotional scars he left me with. Good!

It was not so much my mum's home-knit school jumper that was the issue, but the fact that he told me I had to cross my arms. As you will see from the photo, no one but no one had ever taught me this simple but seemingly prerequisite skill for functioning in the world of the early 1970s, the age of glam rock. I did not know how to fold my arms! I left my 30-second, first photo shoot knowing that I could have done better. I had performed the best approximation of an arm-cross that I could manage, but was aware that it was not going to please any critics of art and form.

At the same time I discovered this picture in my parents' attic, I also stumbled upon a picture of me, taken by my father (I think?) on my fifth birthday. It's an image of me in the family bathroom having stormed off from my own fifth birthday party because my mum was holding some other child's hand in a game of 'Ring a ring o' roses'. I missed the jelly and ice cream (simpler times, folks) because of my tantrum.

Now, my parents were fabulous, but my siblings, being siblings, loved to taunt me with these photographs, but even taking into account these humiliations, the rest of my parents' photograph albums remind me that, on balance, I was privileged to have had a very happy childhood, with so many photographs to look back on with gratitude and joy.

My experiences as a school leader remind me of this perception of my childhood. As a school leader, I made many mistakes along the way, but I would like to think that I got a lot of things right too. There were some exceedingly tough times for my school, and for me personally, which took a huge emotional toll, and yet, with the benefit of some distance and a little added perspective, I choose to look back on those 23 years of leadership with some fondness, remembering the many good times rather than the bad.

For the very most part, teachers enter into leadership roles for the right reasons: to make a positive difference to the lives of children and give them the best possible preparation for adult life in what is increasingly a crazy, messed-up world. On the few occasions that I have known people take on promotions because they are driven by a salary increase, it has rarely gone well! The challenges generally outweigh any financial reward and so you really *do* have to be in it for the right reasons.

So, if most leaders are in it for the right reasons, why is it that sometimes they fall out of love with the job, either temporarily or sometimes permanently?

I recently met up with my friend **Peter Anderton** for a pint and a catch-up as I had not seen him for the best part of a year. Peter is one of the nicest, most decent people you will ever come across. I first met him six years ago when we were both queueing for coffee during a break at a conference and we got talking. At the time, I had just left my headship in order to write and had been invited to give a ten-minute address to a visiting group of secondary school careers advisers. I was contemplating a career in public speaking but was genuinely very anxious about being able to fill a whole ten minutes with content that they would find interesting. What did I know about being a careers adviser? I had been on the brink of declining the offer, but Peter helped me to realise that the best way to get into a cold stream is to jump right in. With his encouragement, I did speak at the university, was at least moderately interesting and gained a new confidence. If you do not step outside your comfort zone, your comfort zone does not stay the same size. It only shrinks. These days, I struggle to speak for anything less than an hour! So, if it had not been for that chance conversation, my career would probably not have taken the turn that it did, I would probably not have taken to writing and you would not be reading this introduction. Thanks, Peter!

As well as being an all-round 'good egg', Peter is something of a leadership boffin, having been a production manager for United Biscuits and organisational development manager for technology giant 3M for nine years. He now runs his own training company, Internal Alignment, and is a TEDx speaker. Peter really knows his stuff. He loves a good Venn diagram and is the only person I know who can explain the principles of good leadership using a packet of chocolate digestives!

I asked Peter why well-intentioned, hard-working leaders in many walks of life do sometimes fall out of love with their job. He thought for a moment and then replied that there are obviously a whole range of factors, depending on the nature of your role and the setting, but there are three big ones that come up time and again:

1 They end up doing fewer and fewer of the things that they joined for and are good at.

2 They often don't feel that the work they are doing is making a real difference and so lack job satisfaction.

3 They experience a feeling of disconnect; the further up the organisation you go, the more isolated you can feel.

Although Peter was not talking specifically about education in schools, his answers resonated very clearly with me and times in my career when I was less happy and fulfilled in my leadership roles.

1 They end up doing fewer and fewer of the things that they joined for and are good at.

I wanted to become a school leader to make a difference to the future prospects of the children and yet I ended up spending less and less time communicating directly with those very children, and more and more time on administration.

2 They often don't feel that the work they are doing is making a real difference and so lack job satisfaction.

Throughout my second headship (an exceptionally large and rapidly expanding primary school), we had significant budgetary challenges, as the local authority funding formula was just not designed to support a school in this unique situation. We won some concessions over the years, but these were hard fought for and very time-consuming and you knew, as local authority budgets were being squeezed, you were probably going to be in exactly the same situation the following year.

3 They experience a feeling of disconnect; the further up the organisation you go, the more isolated you can feel.

Many leadership structures in schools are shaped as pyramids, with a number of people with similar levels of responsibility and pay grades at the bottom, and one person at the top. The higher you progress up that pyramid, the fewer people there are who truly understand the job that you do. For example, I have done a lot of work with school business managers over the last three years, who are experiencing high levels of stress balancing the books and yet often feel isolated in school, partly because some of the decisions they are having to make are unpopular with staff and partly because no one else within the organisation really understands what the job entails. Sound familiar?

The remedy? Well it would be glib of me to suggest that this book will provide all the answers. If that were true, I could make a fortune. (Well actually, probably not, as schools have no money in their budgets!)

However, there are two things that I *do* know.

Firstly, some sense of isolation is inevitable the further up the leadership ladder you go. However, it is *not* entirely unavoidable. Always make the effort to connect with people. Use whole-staff emails sparingly and physically go and see people and communicate. It is the only true way of connecting with people and finding out 'the word on the street'. We have, I am sure, all known leaders who have isolated themselves away in their ivory towers, unaware of what is really going on in the classroom. Even if there is no one else who does your job in school, there will be others doing similar jobs in other schools, so get out there and network, visit another school and join like-minded people in support groups.

Secondly, as a friend and headteacher recently said to me, 'A light that shines twice as brightly shines half as long.' Many teachers are, I suspect, becoming leaders at a younger age than a generation ago. With retirement ages getting later, many will be in leadership roles for longer periods too. The key is not to let the lamp burn out. For sure, it may well flicker at times and that's OK and perfectly normal. Don't beat yourself up about it; we all have our moments of doubt.

As I am writing this, I am in the privileged position of sitting in a cottage in Aberporth in Cardigan Bay, Wales. I do a lot of my writing here. The relative peace and quiet helps me think more clearly and order my thoughts. I have been coming here regularly for 25 years since my children were small, building sandcastles at the seaside and damming the stream that flows effortlessly into the sea. Like many holidaying in the UK, I would set off in the hope of calm seas and sunny weather. However, experience has taught me that, at times, the sea can be more than a little rough to say the least and that you had best be prepared for periods of bad weather.

As I write this, it is a wild and stormy day with 55 mph winds, which are whipping the waves up into tall white horses. Each wave is strong as it crashes onto the sandy beach below me but then the power of the wave diminishes and dissipates among the stones, shells and driftwood. The power of each wave is transitory.

School leadership is like this in so many ways. We enter into it to make a difference to the life opportunities of young people but we do so in at least the hope that our leadership voyage will be blessed with blue skies and calm seas. However, the longer we stay in the job, the more likely we are to encounter high seas and powerful waves. All leaders, over time, will experience challenges that, like waves, seem likely to knock them off course or, worse, overpower them and wash them away.

Some leaders will shy away from the waves, playing things safe and preferring to stay in port where things are a little calmer and less threatening. The water, though relatively undisturbed, soon starts to stagnate and loses its appeal to people passing by.

> *A ship in harbour is safe, but that is not what ships are for.*
>
> John A. Shedd

The leaders I really admire, however, acknowledge that the seas can sometimes be cruel but sail onwards anyway.

The key is being able to ride those waves out until they lose their power.

If you have taken the trouble to read this far then I am sure that you are a leader already or are considering applying for a position. Great – we need people like you! I am also aware that you entered, or are entering, leadership with a higher moral purpose. Again, great; without a compass you can soon lose your way in the myriad decisions you will have to make on a daily basis. However, in order to ride the waves successfully, you actually have to *find*, *hold onto* or occasionally *rediscover* the enjoyment of school leadership.

Over the following pages, I want to explore ten essential elements that, if you can get them right, can significantly help you to ride the waves and avoid the rocks, but more than that, find joy and fulfilment in your job.

Dramatis personae

I don't know about you, but I have read quite a bit of historical fiction over the years, particularly murder mystery novels. One of my favourite authors is Lindsey Davis, who wrote the *Falco* series of novels set in ancient Rome. My difficulty is that I tend to read in quite short bursts and sometimes I just can't remember who a particular character is when they suddenly appear after an absence of a few chapters. Davis very helpfully starts each book with a list of characters who appear in it for quick and easy reference. It's a godsend for someone like me. As various people I know or have interviewed will pop up from time to time throughout this book, I thought that I would adopt the same approach. So, rather like a play script, (I studied drama and education at university), here is a handy guide. The positions are based on each person's role at the time they were interviewed for the book.

Peter Anderton (@peteanderton) TEDx speaker, business leadership expert and all-round nice guy.

Clare Erasmus (@cerasmusteach) Head of Technology and Head of Mental Health and Wellbeing at Brighton Hill Community School, author of *The Mental Health and Wellbeing Handbook for Schools*.

Jonny Mitchell (@MrMitchellCAL) Featured in Channel 4's *Educating Yorkshire* and now Principal at The Co-operative Academy of Leeds.

Patrick Ottley-O'Connor (@ottleyoconnor) Interim Headteacher and an expert in turning schools around. Currently Executive Principal at North Liverpool Academy, Northern Schools Trust.

Rae Snape (@RaeSnape) Headteacher at Spinney Primary School, Cambridge. National Leader of Education and radical optimist.

Hannah Wilson (@Ethical_Leader) Executive Headteacher, Aureus School and Aureus Primary School. Co-founder of #WomenEd.

Angela Browne (@nourishedschool) Interim Deputy CEO, Castle School Education Trust, as featured in the BBC documentary series *School*.

Ritesh Patel (@Mr_Patel100) Director of Learning: Technology and Art, The Leigh UTC and Inspiration.

Lisa Lea-Weston (@TalkingHeadsOak) Supervisor at Talking Heads; supervision for headteachers and dramatherapist.

1 Relationships (part 1): Of pupils, parents and governors

The most important single ingredient in the formula of success is knowing how to get along with people.

Theodore Roosevelt

Now I have two confessions to make in this opening chapter. One is relatively straightforward; the second rather darker one is something I don't think I shared with anyone while I was a senior leader in schools (and I was a senior leader for a very long time!). More of this anon.

OK, confession number one then. When I initially pitched the idea of this book to my editor, Hannah, 'Relationships' was not going to be Chapter 1. It was going to be either Chapter 3 or 4. I don't recall exactly which as I can't locate a copy of that initial pitch. (Honestly, how I ever ran a school of 800 I will never know, as I can barely organise myself these days!) However, when Hannah fed back to me on my proposal, she said that 'Relationships' absolutely needed to be the first chapter because it was the most important of my ten proposed themes. She was right, of course, because if you have poor relationships within a school, you are unlikely to garner a great deal of support and enjoy leadership, which can be very challenging at times. It is worth investing the time to get those relationships as right as you can, accepting the fact that you can never (and nor should you) please all of the people all of the time.

I can remember, in my first term as a teacher, sitting down with my mentor, Dave, and talking about relationships in school. This was my first term review meeting and, with Dave being fairly laid back (as well as hugely supportive), we were holding it in a pub. Dave summarised it for me in one relatively simple diagram.

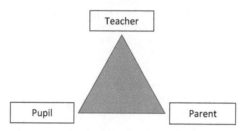

FIGURE 1.1 Relationships in schools (Dave's version).

Not rocket science I know, but in my efforts to deal with classroom management I had underestimated the importance of building relationships with parents and so it made a point to me.

Years later, as the senior leader in school, I came to realise that the beer-mat diagram did not reflect the complexities of a fast-changing education system and so, as an NQT mentor myself now, I drew this on a notepad to show my young colleague who was struggling a little with relationships in school.

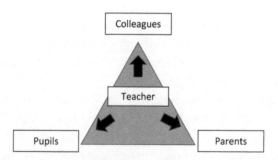

FIGURE 1.2 Relationships in schools (my version).

Still not rocket science, but it was designed to make the point that we should never underestimate what a difference our relationships with colleagues can make, for good or for bad. More on this later.

However, even this does not cover it. Perhaps a more realistic representation of a complex web of relationships would be this:

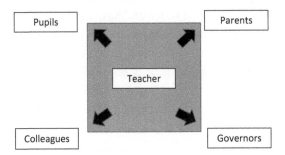

FIGURE 1.3 Relationships in schools (my updated version).

The quality of our relationships in all four areas can significantly add to (or detract from) our enjoyment of leadership. Good relationships can help us through even the stormiest of times.

Relationships with pupils

Few would argue with the fact that the relationship a teacher has with their pupil will have a significant bearing on the child's academic results and, by extension, the success of the school. Finding a connection is so, so important.

The school that I attended between the ages of 11 and 16 did not have a sixth form and for that reason I had to move to another school to study for my A levels. I was a little insecure and found it difficult to establish a new group of friends among people who had, in some cases, been together since the age of five.

It was not helped by the fact that my form tutor, Mr Macrillo, made it appear as if my arrival was a major inconvenience for him. He made it abundantly clear in the first few weeks that he did not like me very much and cut me no slack at all as I tried to adapt to my new surroundings.

Unfortunately, I had elected to study geography, a subject that I had done moderately well at in previous exams. Guess who was the head of geography in school? You got it! None other than Mr Macrillo. He would often make derisory comments about my homework in front of the whole class, and his lessons, to me at least, were interminably dull. I came to dread double geography on a Wednesday afternoon and, sensing that I could do no right, I began to switch off. The more disengaged I became in his beloved subject, the more his irritation with me grew. It was a vicious circle. Having sat through one two-hour exam paper where nothing at all that I had revised came up, it will be of no surprise to you that I got an 'E' at A level.

I am sure that I have my part to play in this, but Mr Macrillo was the adult in the room!

Now given that experience, you might expect that my relationships with my own pupils were always positive and that I was always the adult in the room. Not always so.

Here I come to my second confession of the chapter. This is the one I am really not proud of. In a teaching career spanning more than a quarter of a century, I have talked to hundreds of pupils, thousands I suppose, if you count all the children in the two schools in which I was headteacher. I have taught some fabulous young people and some youngsters who were really quite difficult for a wide variety of reasons, but there have only been three pupils for whom I struggled to find any redeeming features. One of them was a nine-year-old girl called Morag (I have changed her name for obvious reasons).

It was fairly early on in my career and I had a Year 5 class in a large city junior school, the same one where Dave had been my mentor. It was the second half of the autumn term and I had just about got my class where I wanted them. Our headteacher put his head around the door and told me that I should expect a new pupil the following day who was moving into the area, the family having relocated from Scotland.

When she arrived, I tried to be welcoming, honestly I did, but she was rude from the outset, often disobedient, and stirred up a lot of trouble between other members of the class. Afternoon registration was often spent dealing with the aftermath of what had happened over lunchtime in a way that it had not been before her arrival and Morag's name was always in the mix somewhere.

To be honest, my behaviour management strategies were very limited back then, consisting of a) shouting loudly or b) having the pupil stand outside the classroom. Morag spent a lot of time standing outside the classroom.

Once a week, we would all climb aboard the coach and head to the public baths for swimming lessons. I was teaching the more advanced swimmers in the deep end (which is in itself ironic as I am not the strongest of swimmers). Morag was in my group.

This is the really terrible part. I awoke one night from a dream in a cold sweat. I had dreamed that I was standing poolside with my group of eight or so swimmers, all of whom were learning to tread water close to the edge. All of a sudden, Morag started to struggle. Her head disappeared under the water only to reappear again two or three seconds later. As her head disappeared for a second time, her hand reached out to me. I began to bend to offer an outstretched hand and then suddenly I stopped. Morag went under. I presume the lifeguard dived in and saved her but I had woken up and was sitting bolt upright by this stage, so I never did find out!

Told you it was awful! It really deeply shocked me that I could think such a thing, even in my subconscious. I was so fixated on Morag's behaviour and the perceived challenge to my authority that I never really bothered to look beyond that, to try to understand the reasons behind it. She was probably a frightened little girl who had had to up sticks and move with her father's job, leaving her friends and all that was familiar behind her to start over in a new city in a different country, where she knew no one and was struggling to fit in with her classmates. On top of that, she had a teacher who shouted quite a bit and she was made to stand outside her new classroom rather a lot. Very close parallels with my own sixth-form experience, only a few years before. Morag, if you are out there, I apologise for not trying to understand you better. I was the adult in the room.

If I think back to the two other pupils I really struggled to relate to, they were also from this early period of my career. Perhaps I got better at empathy as I developed as teacher and leader. I certainly got better at building healthy relationships with pupils.

Clare Erasmus is Head of Faculty and Head of Mental Wellbeing at Brighton Hill Community School in Basingstoke. I first met her in 2016 at Pedagoo Hampshire, organised by Martyn Reah, founder of #teacher5aday. She is passionate about both teacher and pupil wellbeing and has written for the *TES*.

Clare says that building positive relationships with pupils can be compared with doing a jigsaw. It takes time to build a complete picture and we shouldn't give up when something doesn't seem to fit. It is about building trust and this requires confidence and often a great deal of resilience. It is all about the **C**s, she says.

Connect *and* care

Remember that pupils have a background and life outside of school and that they are slowly carving out their identities. They will often get things wrong but you need to show that you are still concerned for, and interested in, their wellbeing regardless.

For pupils who find it hard to engage with school, try to find one thing that they are interested in outside of school and try to connect around that. Try to get them to join in an extracurricular activity or create something around their interests, and spend time talking to them without judgement. When pupils do make mistakes, help them to navigate their way out of the situation. Don't just punish them.

Consistency

Be as consistent as you can, particularly around behaviour. Fluctuating expectations will cause confusion and potentially erode trust. Always greet your students and be consistent in treating them with dignity and respect.

Challenge

Try to make your lessons accessible and relevant. If they are not, pupils will be unlikely to engage and this is likely to undermine your relationship with them. Your teaching needs to feel relevant to the world they live in. Make sure the classroom environment is both safe and stimulating and that the level of challenge allows them to make marginal gains.

Make sure pupils know that you care about what you are teaching and that you want them to do well. If you invest time in them in lessons, they are more likely to invest in you.

Communicate

Show students that you value their contributions and efforts. Perhaps tell them at the start of the lesson what you were impressed by in the last one. Showcase their achievements with verbal feedback in front of the class. Praise publicly but reprimand privately. Assessment scales are just one aspect of achievement. Don't lose sight that kindness, helpfulness, truthfulness and resilience are all important too. Reflect that in your praise and highlight any achievements for other members of staff to see, as well as in assemblies and newsletters.

Calm

Teaching is hard work and can be very stressful at times. Try to manage your stress levels as they will impact negatively on your relationship with pupils. Talk to someone. Don't bottle things up if you are feeling under pressure and feel like you might be taking things out on a pupil; step back and pause or this will actually set you back in the long run. Be prepared to apologise. It shows you are only human and can help to strengthen your relationship.

And lastly…

Collaborate

Avoid clashes becoming personal. Connect with other staff who have had dealings with the pupil, such as other or previous teachers, find out the bigger picture, and what works and what does not. Be consistent as a staff team and create a coordinated effort to find opportunities for the pupil to succeed and feel valued.

If relationships are like jigsaws, we should not abandon them when something does not seem to fit. Instead, we should stare at the board, search for the missing pieces and keep trying until we can complete the whole picture.

Clare Erasmus (2018)

Time to reflect

Consider a current pupil you might have a difficult relationship with. Now consider the advice above. Is there anything you might consider doing differently?

Relationships with parents

There is an old adage in school leadership that suggests that ten per cent of parents can take up 50 per cent of your time. To be honest, the percentages vary according to whom you speak to, but the principle remains the same; a small number of parents have the ability to make or break your day, week, term or year.

A friend of mine works as a nurse in our local hospital. He says that they begin every shift with a plan of action but, within the first hour, some event will happen that will blow them off course, dealing with issues that they could not have anticipated only a few hours previously. This rang true to me in terms of leadership in schools. As a head I would consult my desk diary on a daily basis to see what the day had in store (assuming I could read my own handwriting, which has never been more than a scrawl) and in my mind I would prepare a mental plan of the day. With 800 pupils on roll, it was almost inevitable that a phone call, letter or visit from a parent would then blow me somewhat off course and lead to me dealing with issues that I could not have anticipated when I woke from my slumber that morning. My ability and that of other members of the senior leadership team to resolve these issues quickly would depend, to no small extent, on the relationship that we had with the parents. Those with whom we had developed a close working relationship would trust our word and our ability to resolve the issue they had raised. These were often issues to do with friendships, fallouts and suggestions of bullying. Those parents with whom we struggled to develop a working relationship were often the ones who would be quick to believe their darling offspring's version of events without question. Inevitably these were the issues that tended to be the most time-consuming as we had to gather the evidence to confront the fact that their child might not have told the truth, the whole truth and nothing but the truth!

So, on a purely practical level, it makes sense to engage with parents (although I have met and worked with school leaders who would work hard to keep parents at arm's length!).

Engaging with parents makes a lot of sense on many other levels too.

Firstly, the manner in which we communicate with parents tends to have a bearing on how much parents involve themselves in their child's learning at home. Schools that are quick to communicate bad tidings, such as poor behaviour or academic progress, but are slow to communicate and celebrate good news, such as small steps of progress, will often find themselves in adversarial relationships where the school is perceived to be the enemy and parents begin to worry about their parenting skills and their ability to help their child in the home environment.

Secondly, while some parents (and indeed some whole communities) are hard to engage, many parents do benefit by getting ideas from their child's school about how best to support them and by demystifying the school's curriculum and the way that it operates. This in turn builds trust and a greater understanding for the parents of the important role that they have to play in their child's education.

Thirdly, I believe that there are real advantages for pupils when their parents become involved and there is good communication between home and school. Children are less likely to 'play one side off against the other' and there is improved motivation for hard work as well as homework, good behaviour and attendance.

Fourthly, school leaders and teachers in general benefit from communication. There is no doubt that it takes time and effort, but then most things worth having do! The payback is that teachers can concentrate more on actual teaching in the classroom, leaders can spend more time concentrating on the myriad challenges that they face on a day-to-day basis, and be blown off course less of the time, and parents who are engaged tend to have a more positive view of teachers (which helps, to no small extent, with morale) and of the school (which certainly helps when the time comes for the inspectors to visit – as I write this a close friend has just texted to say that they have received that call!).

Examples of good communication with parents include:

1 Open evenings.

2 Parent consultation evenings. All the technology in the world cannot replace open and honest conversations between staff and parents, where both sides share information.

3 Subject workshops, e.g. maths and how to support your children with calculation strategies. Short videos explaining methodology on the school website can also be a powerful resource for engaging with parents.

4 Inviting parents in to work alongside their children for a morning (bear in mind I come from a primary background!).

5 Regular newsletters.

6 Use of social media, e.g. Facebook and Twitter, to start conversations and share good news. Social media is also an effective way of keeping parents up to date when pupils are out on school visits or on residential trips. Parents worry less!

7 Blogs to share news of particular year groups or departments, as well as one from the head.

8 Phone calls home for good reasons!

9 Inviting parents to achievement assemblies.

10 Home–school journals that highlight any behavioural issues but, at least as importantly, the pupil's successes and achievements.

11 Parent forums that help to shape school policies on a range of issues.

12 Annual school calendars on the school website, which allow parents to plan well in advance for special events and INSET days.

This list is far from exhaustive, and I am sure you could add to it with examples of good practice from your own context. As with most things in teaching, one of the frustrations is that there is always something more that you could do. If you are not careful, you could end up spending so much time trying to communicate with parents that you have no time to perform any of the other functions of a leader or manager. Equally, placing excessive demands on teaching staff to be ringing parents every five minutes, for example, is unrealistic and likely to win you very few friends! (No, I am not suggesting that as a leader you should be friends with everyone and currying favour. However, realistic expectations are key to trust and respect.) So, the key here is to be effective and look for quick wins that will make a big impact with parents.

The five golden rules

1 **Be proactive.** Introduce yourself and your expectations at the earliest opportunity to new parents through a letter or a meeting.

2 **Be timely.** If you do have an issue to discuss with parents that is bad news, contact them before their child speaks to them with their own version of events. Timely intervention will help lead to a timely resolution. Delays tend to generate frustration, which can then lead to other problems.

3 **Be consistent and frequent.** Within bounds of reasonableness, provide frequent, ongoing feedback about how pupils are performing.

4 **Be clear.** Make sure your communications are useful. Without patronising parents, make sure your messages are in language they will understand.

5 **Follow things through.** Trust and relationships will only be built if parents see that you actually do what you said you would do.

Time to reflect

How do you as a *school* communicate to parents:

- your curriculum and what their child is studying?

- their child's progress and accomplishments?

- what they can do at home to help their child's education?

Now thinking about yourself as a *leader*:
- How does your school communicate your visions and values?

- How do you involve parents in the shaping of that vision?

- What alignment would an inspector find between your own view of the vision and values of the school and that of a parent?

- How might a change in the way you communicate improve that alignment?

Relationships with governors

The organisation of schools is becoming ever more varied and complex and so the way that they are governed is also changing. I will confess that in 23 years of school leadership, all my own personal experience has been in the context of local-authority-run schools, where the model was one school with one governing body. While for many of you reading this book this may appear an outdated model, I believe the principles of developing and maintaining a positive relationship with governors, in whatever form, remain largely the same.

I have worked with four governing bodies as a school leader, three of them as a headteacher. When I think of it that does not sound like an awful lot, *but* I worked in two of those schools for long periods (13 years and ten years) and as such I saw many governors from different backgrounds come through and exit the revolving door that made up the governing body. I was lucky, by and large. I liked most of them and established a good rapport, largely down to two factors:

1   Most of them were in it for the right reasons, i.e. to support schools and create the best opportunities and outcomes for the pupils within it.*

2   They respected my professional integrity and the integrity of the staff I worked with.**

*I do recall one parent governor getting herself elected and then bringing a proposal to her very first meeting under AOB, and without warning me: for her existing business to open a before-school care provision on the school site. I was fuming, and to be fair, most of the rest of the governing body were too. Talk about an ulterior motive!

**I have experienced governors who, while largely supportive of the school, had issues with a particular member of staff, usually based on their child's own experience with that teacher. They would, on occasion, have to be reminded that, as a governor, they needed to maintain a degree of objectivity and that their authority was as part of a whole governing body. (Therefore, asking to observe said member of staff teach would not be appropriate!)

At the end of the day, governors are volunteers. They don't have to do the job and most of them will have busy working lives outside of school. In my experience, many are ready to hold the school to account and challenge the senior leadership where appropriate. That is fine – that is what they are meant to do. However, few are quick to challenge the way that the governing body itself is run and organised. For most, this will be their first experience of being a governor so they tend to accept the ways and systems as being the norm. Why wouldn't they? They have little or nothing to benchmark themselves against. Some of the systems can be archaic and not fit for purpose. My advice would be to assert as much authority as possible, as early as possible, to shape the way the body to whom you are accountable operates.

When I took up my second headship in 2003, things were a bit of a mixed bag. Under the leadership of my predecessor the school had expanded rapidly, amalgamated on one site and hung on to its village school ethos. No small feat! Hats off to my predecessor, for whom I have the greatest respect.

However, there was a huge budget deficit, largely associated with funding catching up with pupil numbers. While applying for the position,

I had understood that the local authority was comfortable with the situation, accepting that when pupil numbers plateaued, the situation would be resolved. On the second or third day in post, I received a letter from the local authority informing me that I needed to turn the deficit around within 12 to 18 months. In common with most schools, 80 per cent of our budget was tied up in staffing. While it was true that the school was generously resourced, certainly in comparison with my previous headship, there was no way of reducing outgoings without cutting staff. Not an enviable announcement to have to make in your first few days in a new school! Added to this, the school's deputy headteacher had been seconded as acting head of another school. Further complicating the situation was that, on the back of all this, the chair of governors resigned within my first few days.

Within every adversity is the possibility of opportunity. The governing body had so many subcommittees to which the head was expected to attend, all of which took place in the evening. Having survived a short period of this punishing schedule and trying to turn up fresh as a daisy each and every day, I told the new chair of governors that I could not continue like this and proposed a slimmed-down committee structure: that we would all meet prior to a main governors' meeting. Clearly, I could not attend all of them. (I have a few talents in my repertoire, but omnipresence is not one of them.) Instead, I would deploy a member of the senior leadership team that was best suited to the agenda for that particular subcommittee. The chair of each committee then reported back on their meeting as an agenda item in the main governors' meeting.

Back in November, I delivered a keynote speech on resilience and stress management to around 200 staff from two secondary schools in Leeds. I had been booked by a fantastic deputy head who had seen me speak at a TeachMeet in Batley in Yorkshire a few months previously. I turned up at the Co-operative Academy of Leeds, and Caroline, the deputy, introduced me to their head, who was sitting on the registration desk smiling and joking with people as they arrived. I did the classic double take as I realised that it was **Jonny Mitchell**, the head from Channel 4's *Educating Yorkshire*. We got on really well and have been talking ever since.

He explained to me his frustration that as a head, new in post, papers were being tabled at the actual governors' meeting without anybody having had the opportunity to read them before the meeting itself. As a consequence, reading time had to be allowed within the meeting and participants had little or no time to reflect on the contents before it was time to make a decision. Meetings, as a result, dragged on to say the least. Jonny quickly put in place measures to ensure that papers were submitted in a timely fashion well before any meeting and with an expectation that all participants would have read them, and reflected upon them, in advance. He also set a time limit on meetings. Sage advice!

For your own sanity, set your stall out!

Look, if you have read any of my other books you will see that I didn't always get things right and I think that the notion of the school leader as a superhero is fundamentally flawed. Looking back, I think that one of the things I got wrong in terms of governance is that I adopted the same approach as I did to staffing. I aimed for a collegiate approach. We are all in this together, if you like. As a leader, I came to realise that I needed people who were strong in the areas where I was weaker, such as finance (I was competent, but not strong – Excel spreadsheets still send a shiver down my spine). Sometimes through chance and sometimes through purposeful action, for example co-opting parents with particular skillsets, I was able to build a governing team who, from their professional lives, had expertise in finance, human resources, buildings, health and safety, and so on. I had the director of a major UK car manufacturing plant advising someone who was, and still is, relatively poor at numbers (i.e. me) on finance! It was great. We worked together, pulled together and sometimes even laughed together as a governing body, just as we did as a staff. Sounds great, doesn't it? The difficulty was, and this eventually showed in one inspection, that in creating this collegiate ideal, I did not always equip the governors as well as I could with the tools to challenge the school properly and my leadership personally.

A bit of insecurity on my part? I would have to confess, yes. Few leaders do not doubt themselves at times and those who don't probably should!

As I write this, I realise that Hannah, my editor, was correct. Relationships are so important. I have reached my word count on this chapter on relationships and not yet touched on the relationships between senior leaders and their colleagues. So, and not as planned (as we've discovered, I am not the most organised person on this planet!), let's deal with the issue of inter-staff relationships in a whole new chapter!

Summary

- Good-quality relationships with pupils, parents, colleagues and governors will pay dividends. Invest time in developing them all.
- However challenging a pupil's behaviour, always be the adult in the room.
- When considering your relationships with pupils, remember the seven Cs:

Connect – Care – Consistency – Challenge – Communicate – Calm – Collaborate.

- How we communicate with parents will have a strong bearing on how they will engage with their child's learning at home.
- Engage with parents, even (and perhaps especially) the ones you would rather keep at arm's length.
- Keep a balance between communicating the positives as well as the negatives.
- Remember the five golden rules of communicating with parents:

Be proactive – Be timely – Be consistent and frequent – Be clear – Follow things through.

- When working with governors, don't lose sight of the fact that at the end of the day, they are volunteers.
- Set your stall out in terms of structure, frequency and duration of meetings.
- While getting on with your governors is important, make sure that you give them the tools to challenge the school and your leadership.

2 Relationships (part 2): Colleagues

Each relationship nurtures a strength or weakness within you.

Mike Murdock

Of all the factors that can affect the success of a school, one of the most critical is the relationship between a leader and their colleagues. I am convinced that success can be predicted by how well the staff work (and indeed play) together. Successful school leaders have the ability to foster and maintain human relationships, enabling their team to achieve extraordinary things on a regular basis.

It is often said that we do not truly appreciate something until it is gone.

My two substantive headships were very different affairs. In my first headship, I took over a school of around 400 pupils at which I had been the deputy head for eight years. There was no such thing back then as leadership and management time nor planning, preparation and assessment time (PPA). I was first and foremost a classroom teacher who performed most leadership functions outside of the pupils' school day.

As such, I knew the majority of parents and had taught many of their children. I had good relationships with members of the governing body as I had served as a staff governor since arriving, on secondment, eight years previously. Indeed, they had quietly but actively encouraged me to apply for the headship when our much-admired head, Pam Underwood, retired. I knew all the staff and, working in a 70s-built, semi-open-plan school, I had taught cheek by jowl with many of them. These relationships were positive in the vast majority of cases, and as I started my first substantive headship (I had done a couple of stints as acting head of both my own school and a small village primary that had gone into special measures), I felt a tremendous sense of goodwill. The whole school community wanted me to do well.

Nonetheless, after I had spent five successful years there as head, I did start to experience itchy feet and was very conscious of the fact that I had now been at the school, albeit in different roles, for 13 years. Just as television actors worry about becoming typecast, I worried that, if I didn't make a career move soon, I might become trapped. I began to look around and found an opportunity at a primary school that was expanding very rapidly and that the local authority planned to expand from 150 to 600 on roll (when I eventually left, ten years later, we had over 800 pupils, but that is by the by). I applied and much to my surprise, as I was still quite young, I was appointed. I was greatly excited but can clearly remember my first visit post-interview when I looked at the staff photo board in the entrance hall. There were already twice as many staff members as I had experienced in my previous role, and with each visit, I would try to memorise (and memory has never been my strong point!) a row of photographs and the corresponding names. I do not think, as a leader, I have ever felt so much at sea as I did during those first few days in post. The chair of governors had resigned (for personal reasons – not in protest at my appointment, let's be clear!), the deputy head had been seconded by the local authority as acting head to another school, I had a massive budget deficit to sort and as such was the bearer of much bad news around staffing. The support and relationships that I had enjoyed, but largely taken for granted, in my first headship seemed a lifetime away. I felt a crushing sense of isolation.

If you are in a school leadership role for any length of time, you will experience difficulties and traumas; those waves will inevitably come crashing into shore.

Never underestimate the power of good relationships with your staff to carry you through difficult times.

For many of us, I suspect, our closest friendships lie outside of work. However, the ability to develop strong connections within the work environment can help to carry us through even the hardest of times. Tal Ben-Shahar and Angus Ridgway talk about this in their 2017 book, *The Joy of Leadership*. They suggest that having a friend in the workplace correlates with increased levels of job satisfaction and the resulting lower turnover of staff. In other words, staff are more likely to stay in a place where they have a good time and enjoy strong social connections. Unfortunately for school leaders, there are many roadblocks that can stand in the way of such positive relationships, for example:

1 Most leadership structures are like pyramids; the higher up you go, the fewer people there are who do a comparative job within the school, so fewer people actually understand what it is that you do, which can leave leaders feeling isolated.

2 School leaders are under immense pressure and as such there are real time constraints. Investing in relationships requires time.

3 Technology has changed the way we communicate as leaders and it becomes far easier to send whole-department or even whole-school staff emails than to connect with people individually.

In our lives outside school we have a broad spectrum of choice in the people we spend our time with. People whom we 'click with' we will devote time to and develop a relationship with. If that relationship then turns sour, we generally have some ability to cut that person out of our lives or at least reduce the amount of contact we have with them. The school environment provides us with a much smaller pool of people with whom to connect and will invariably contain at least one person with whom we would not choose to spend our time under almost any other circumstances! Notwithstanding the school holidays, most leaders work very long hours. Your happiness and to some degree the success of your school depend on your ability to form and maintain healthy relationships with staff.

Ben-Shahar and Ridgway (2017) argue that the two most important relationship enablers for leaders are authenticity and positivity.

Authenticity

We can all struggle a little with identity at times. Pressures from above to do things that we know in our heart of hearts are not in pupils' or staff's best interests, eagerness to demonstrate competence and authority, along with a tendency to want to please others can all get in the way of the leader's ability to be their natural self. Being you is not always an easy task, particularly if you are under pressure.

Becoming a leader is synonymous with becoming yourself. It's precisely that simple and also that difficult.

Warren Bennis (2009)

Time to reflect

When was the last time you felt under pressure as a leader to be something that you were not?

How did it make you feel?

What did you do to address the situation?

I delivered a session for the Bath and North East Somerset branch of the NAHT last week. I have worked with them before (it's always great to get asked back somewhere!) and I was talking about the importance of building trust between leaders and other staff in school. I went through my top ten tips (you can find these in my book *Ten Traits of Resilience*) and asked the participants to consider what they would add to that list. When I took some feedback, a headteacher from the back of the room said, 'You must always be authentic, otherwise nobody will believe a word you say.' It struck a chord, because she was absolutely right. To be authentic means to be genuine, real and not a copy of any other leader. Talking to **Jonny Mitchell** exclusively for this book, he told me that he had evolved his leadership style by reflecting on the best elements of leaders he had known, while also considering leadership behaviours that he had observed and thought to himself, 'I wouldn't do it like that.' And for most of us I think that is what we do.

We try to emulate the best qualities of the leaders who have inspired us, rule out the behaviours that have annoyed, upset and disappointed us and mix these with our own visions and values – a unique concoction that makes us what we are and what we should always strive to stay true to.

Richard Boston (2014), in his book *ARC Leadership*, states that authenticity is heavily tied in with personal values, so to be seen to be authentic, others need to be able to align actions with our personal values.

Time to reflect

Try summing up your values in a statement of no more than 30 words.

If you asked another member of staff, what would they say about your values?

How close an alignment would there be between their views and yours?

The perception of our authenticity depends not only on the clarity we have regarding our own values but also on how clearly we communicate those values to our colleagues.

Positivity

While authenticity should be a high priority, it is not enough on its own. I am sure some of the great dictators of the last century were probably authentic and true to themselves. Authenticity needs to go hand in hand with trust. The degree to which staff will trust you is based on their perception of your competence (i.e. your achievements, track record and the ability to get things done in a timely fashion) and your character (i.e. their perception of your benevolence and wishing to do well by the pupils and staff for anything other than selfish gain). Kindness along with positivity and a concern for others are critical for healthy staff (and indeed pupil) relationships.

Ben-Shahar and Ridgway (2017) argue that when we have high levels of authenticity but are not being particularly pleasant to colleagues, we are acting as drivers; in other words, we are highly motivated and task-focused but are paying less attention to the emotional needs of the people around us. We are just trying to get things done and out of the way.

On the other hand, we can fall into the trap of having high levels of positivity and low levels of authenticity. This can be characterised as weak leadership where we become the crowd-pleaser but equally it can also characterise a leader who is manipulative and using flattery to curry favour and get their own way.

The worst position to be in as a leader is if you are low on both authenticity and positivity!

An unusual state of mind, because there's no advantage to being both false and mean – but we all have our moments.

Ben-Shahar and Ridgway (2017)

Most of us would like to think that we are both positive and authentic. People who are these things are generally regarded with warmth and are seen to be both popular and gregarious. None of us are like that all the time but, when we are, we are being the best version of ourselves as a leader. We are motivated to get things done, we care about the methodology of how they are done, and we empower others within the school. It's a win–win scenario.

So how can we feel that way more of the time? I think it is down to a number of factors.

Recognise the achievements of others

I can remember a colleague once telling me that, as a young teacher, keen to impress and make a mark, she had organised a science and technology fair within her school. Some members of staff were a little reticent at first but eventually got behind the idea. Like a snowball rolling down the hill, it gathered momentum. Other schools became involved, they were able to get some commercial sponsorship (which at the time was quite unusual) and the local press became very interested. This in turn led to a number of

VIPs from the local authority turning up on the day to have their picture taken. The school had not enjoyed such positive publicity in years. And yet, when the story appeared in the local paper, there was no mention of my colleague at all. Instead, there was a quote from her headteacher, who had had little or nothing to do with the project and had been one of the initial sceptics. My colleague moved on shortly afterwards.

There are two things people want more than sex and money: recognition and praise.
Mary Kay Ash

Always, always treat people as you wish to be treated. The best school leaders I've worked with did not seek personal glory. Instead they went out of their way to recognise the achievements of others, giving credit where credit was due. Effective leaders seldom have the monopoly on good ideas but encourage others to come forward with theirs. Be open in staff meetings and say, 'This was a great idea and full credit to Dale (or Yasmin or whoever) for coming up with it.'

Time to reflect

As a senior leadership team, how do you recognise the achievements of others?

- In a private way?

- In a public way?

Show gratitude

Saying thank you is so important and yet in our busy lives we can all be guilty of taking things for granted and not expressing our gratitude. By not saying thank you we lose a degree of respect and people start to view us differently. It can make the difference between staff being willing to go that extra mile for you and for the school, or not. Successful schools live on goodwill. Lose that and you lose a crucial factor in school development.

With recruitment and retention a real issue, it has been my experience over many years that people tend to want to stay in environments where they feel valued, recognised and listened to.

Five tips for showing gratitude

1 **Say thank you often.** Leaders rarely succeed without the support of the team that they lead. Every thank you is a credit in someone's personal ledger with you. Keep your accounts in credit where at all possible.

2 **Be genuine.** People are quick to see through flannel and it undermines your credibility as a leader.

3 **Be specific.** Make sure that people know exactly what it is you are thanking them for. It's nice to hear 'Good job!' but 'The presentation you gave to governors was brilliant. It bowled them over!' works far better.

4 **Be timely.** It is no good thanking people weeks after the event. The moment has passed and so will have the impact of your gratitude.

5 **Put your gratitude in writing where you can.** It increases the impact of your recognition. I have known thank-you cards and even simple sticky notes stay up in teachers' classrooms for months and years.

Patrick Ottley-O'Connor once reminded me of Roland Barthes' quote that a good leader is not a hero but a hero-maker. **Make this your mantra.**

Celebrate

Having said all this, it is not solely the job of leaders to recognise success. Rather, it is the job of school leaders to help to establish a culture of recognition. Most schools, in my experience, are pretty good at recognising the achievements of the students through reward systems and special assemblies, but pay less attention to the celebration of individual staff, year groups, faculties and so on.

Some schools have a briefing meeting on a Friday morning where they celebrate the successes of the week, leaving staff in a positive frame of mind as they head into the weekend. We need to share success stories regularly, where saying thank you becomes ingrained in the interactions between all staff, but as with all things, we need as leaders to model the behaviour we would like to see.

Kouzes and Posner (2017), in their book *The Leadership Challenge*, talk about celebrations as being 'like the concert is to the score'. They help to express the vision and values of a school and help to bring staff together behind a set of ideals.

[Celebrations] are like the punctuation marks that make sense of the passage of time; without them, there are no beginnings and endings. Life becomes an endless series of Wednesdays.

Kouzes and Posner (2017)

However, they also caution that such celebrations should be genuinely in line with those centrally held values and staff's commitment towards them, otherwise they lack any real authenticity and devalue the credibility of the celebration and, indeed, that of the leader themselves. Celebrating together adds real heart to the school community and helps forge connections that can carry you through the toughest of times. It can also reduce the likelihood of developing an 'us and them' culture that permeates the corridors of some schools, creating a toxic environment.

Respect

Successful school leaders build and maintain productive working relationships not by accident but because they both earn respect and offer it back where appropriate. We all display leadership qualities to varying degrees. (It is hard to imagine any teacher successfully engaging students without demonstrating some leadership qualities!) However, we are all there on something of a sliding scale. So, let's imagine a scale of one to ten in which one would be a very low level of natural leadership and ten would be very high. Let's imagine then that my natural leadership level is around an eight.

For a number of years, I sat on various working parties for what was then the National College of School Leadership (in many ways a forerunner of The Chartered College of Teaching). I loved it and felt privileged in some small way to help shape national policy. But any inaugural meeting of a group was always a most interesting affair as you had a group of experienced school leaders with high levels of leadership trying to agree on what should be done and how we should go about it. I was often quite quiet in these early meetings; it was not long after I had returned to work as a head after a period of absence due to work-related stress. I guess I kept my head down a little, partly because I recognised I was often not the most articulate person in the room (and I had developed a tendency to stammer), but also because I was weighing up the politics that were being played out. In such situations I would subconsciously be looking for somebody whose leadership level appeared higher than mine (i.e. nine or ten) to emerge as group leader. If that person's leadership style was inclusive and non-aggressive, I would most likely get behind them and bring my own skills and abilities to the table. What I wouldn't be doing, however, was throwing my weight behind somebody I judged to have leadership skills that were more like a five or six in comparison with my eight. Perhaps my opinion would be reached erroneously and on the basis of limited information, but we tend to follow our gut instinct. In any initial meeting of a working party, many different ideas would be tabled and the group would pull in different directions as people vied to have their views heard, but sooner or later it became clear who the strongest leaders in the group were and people would start to follow them.

Sound familiar? This phenomenon is nothing new. Dr John C. Maxwell (2007), an internationally recognised leadership expert, speaker and author, refers to this as 'The Law of Respect'. People will naturally align themselves with stronger leaders than themselves. We can grow our leadership skills over time but there is little doubt in my mind that some of this is innate.

I worked for a head once whom I liked, but every day did seem a bit like Groundhog Day. It was pre-OFSTED, which makes things a little different, but you did often feel as though, if you fell asleep and awoke 20 years later – Rip Van Winkle style – very little would have actually changed. His successor ruffled a few feathers to be sure, but he had a real strategic vision for the school and its place within the community, and I bought into him big time! He was a leader I could really follow. He had a natural leadership ability to my mind and, when he talked about vision, I was genuinely quite excited as a 20-something-year-old teacher who had kind of drifted into the job.

However, let us not confuse drive and true leadership. I have met a handful of autocratic school leaders who seem to rely on tactics of bullying and intimidation in order to get what they want. For obvious reasons I am not going to name them here! As a tactic for managing people it may arguably bring about some short-term gains but it creates a toxic environment where it becomes difficult to retain staff, although they may feel trapped for fear of what references they might receive. As Maxwell points out, this is not real leadership. People follow leaders voluntarily – not because they are frightened into it. They will genuinely only really follow people whom they truly respect in school. If someone respects you as a person, then they will come to admire you. If they respect you as a leader, then they will choose to follow you.

Respect is reciprocal:

FIGURE 2.1 Reciprocal respect

One measure of leadership is the caliber of people who choose to follow you.

Dennis A. Peer

The pace of change in school is exponential and time is rarely a leader's friend. If you have been in post for a while, you have probably had the opportunity to invest time in getting to know your staff, their strengths, areas for development and interests. Good leaders see this as a genuine investment of their time. However, if you are new in post, you rarely have such a luxury. You need to build relationships quickly, earning respect by modelling it yourself and inspiring people to *want* to follow you.

So how can we gain that respect from the staff we work with? Here are six by no means exhaustive suggestions.

1. Set the standards you want to see

Actions always speak louder than words. People will only respect and follow you if they see that what you actually do around school matches up to any rhetoric. In other words, you need to 'walk the walk' as well as 'talk the talk'. Model a good work ethic consistently. Many of us will have encountered school leaders who talk a good game, but actually, as time wears away the veneer they have put into place, there is very little of substance and they soon lose credibility. A good work ethic helps to demonstrate that you are trustworthy both inside and out.

2. Model a good work–life balance

If you are consistently the first person in the building in the morning and the last to leave at night, you are sending a clear message. *I work long hours and so should you.* If you regularly send emails or text messages to colleagues during the evening or at weekends, you are sending a clear message. *I am working right now and so should you be.* If, on the other hand, you talk about the holidays you are planning, your own kids' sports days that you are going to and how Tuesday is your go-home-early night or Thursday is the morning when you arrive a little later to work, then you start to send out a rather different message. *I believe in looking after my own wellbeing and it is important to me that you invest in your own wellbeing.* I know which kind of a leader I would rather follow.

Time to reflect

What kind of signals do you send staff about their wellbeing?

- Intentionally?

- Unintentionally?

- What might you do differently to communicate those priorities more clearly?

3. Be courageous

Success never goes hand in hand with stagnation in my experience. Without trial and error and a degree of risk-taking as a leader, you are likely to become predictable and complacent, and ultimately stagnate. This is dangerous, because over time schools will become just like their leaders (for good or for bad). Risk-taking is about pushing yourself until you are operating outside your own comfort zone. While the familiar often feels comfortable, most people admire a little risk-taking from their leaders, as long as it is tempered with good judgment of course – choose your battles wisely but allow yourself to take a step that might feel uncomfortable at first. Comfort zones only expand if we step outside them from time to time.

Even some of the most successful school leaders I have interviewed in the last few years do recognise that at the core of their risk-taking is a sense of fear. It is often a fear of failing pupils, staff and the wider community. Or it can be fear of losing face and damaged credibility (all leaders have some kind of an ego!). Taking risks means confronting these fears and challenges and still having the courage to move forward towards a greater good. However, the other side of this admirable quality is, of course, being able to admit when we have made mistakes. No follower within a school context will truly believe their leaders to be infallible, but they will expect them to be honest!

4. Be just

There is no quicker way I know to gain respect than to put right historical wrongs. I knew a head once – we will call him Stephen. He ran a large special school with a lot of support staff. Stephen was very much on the wind-down to retirement after many successful years as a school leader. He made some poor decisions in the final months in my humble view. I won't go into details here, but it was to do with consolidation of temporary contracts into permanent ones mixed in with some pay-grading issues. In fairness to Stephen, he was trying to tie up loose ends, and the governors, somewhat used to following his recommendations, approved these recommendations. The rationale behind those decisions was a

Relationships (part 2)

little dubious and caused a lot of resentment in some quarters of the staff, and union reps were involved, but little was actually resolved before his departure.

Emma, his successor, quickly saw the injustice of what had happened and, despite the financial implications and without casting aspersions about Stephen's huge abilities and significant legacy, set about putting the injustices right. She won respect and followers very quickly, among both the staff and the governors. She had nailed her leadership colours to the mast at speed and had shown herself to be someone they could trust.

5. Have their backs

Good school leaders work hard to achieve an almost impossible ideal: that is, to put measures in place to let staff get on with the jobs they are trained to do.

These efforts include striving to ensure that they have the resources to do the job effectively. I spent *so* many hours sitting in finance meetings with representatives of our local authority trying to secure changes to a funding formula that was largely set up to do the best by small village primaries to the detriment of larger schools (running a primary school with over 800 on roll was also not without its challenges!). However, the financial challenges for almost all schools have become so much greater in recent years.

I know **Patrick Ottley-O'Connor** sees the job of school leaders as 'barrier removal operatives', i.e. it is their job to remove the obstacles that get in the way of teachers teaching great lessons. That might be removing excessive expectations of lesson planning or erecting walls in spaces devised by well-meaning architects who still think that open-plan spaces are a great idea (but have never taught a lesson to 30-plus easily distractible young people in their lives!).

But a third way of having the backs of the staff that you lead is to show loyalty. You can do this in the good times with recognition and praise, but in the bad times by acting as a buffer or a 'human shield' between outside distractions and those who are 'at the chalk face'.

> *They protect their people from red tape, meddlesome executives, nosy visitors, unnecessary meetings, and a host of other insults, intrusions and time wasters.*
>
> Robert I. Sutton (2010)

The above is a business quote, I know, but I think we can all connect with it in schools on one level or another.

This notion of having staff's backs and showing loyalty also extends to people who make mistakes. Goodness only knows, most people are sufficiently self-aware to know that they will commit some 'howlers' in their time. I know a secondary deputy head who, a few years ago, made a mess-up with timetabling at the start of the year. Easily done. (I am not judging – I could not do timetabling if my life depended on it. I am creative but *so* scatty.) It caused chaos in the early days of September, almost to rival the changes to the new rail timetable in the UK in 2018, when hundreds of trains were cancelled because trains and crews were not in the right places. Her head was right behind her and stayed so throughout those difficulties.

The degree to which staff will respect and ultimately follow us is in inverse proportion to how quickly they perceive we will 'throw them under the bus' when the 's**t hits the fan'.

It *will* always do this from time to time. I have sat through many meetings defending staff with parents (usually), governors (sometimes) and inspection teams (occasionally), feeling a little uncomfortable in the process and yet knowing it was the right thing to do.

And yet…

6. Have those difficult conversations

Oh my word… I don't think I will be on my own in saying that this is one of the most difficult elements of school leadership. Most of us like harmony and it is easy to put off those conversations about poor performance, particularly when you really like the person involved.

Unfortunately, as Patrick says, 'Bad news is not like fine wine; it does not improve with age.' It is a little like the lady I keep bumping into in Tesco (other supermarkets are available). She clearly knows *me* and we have exchanged pleasantries for the last two years. I have a shocking memory and I have absolutely no idea who she is. I should have asked her the first time we met but I pretended I knew. Now the moment has passed and I have to struggle through toe-curling conversations. It was like that with Annie, a teacher I worked with a few years back.

> Annie was great with the kids and with parents. Brilliant at resolving bullying issues and the like. She also ran loads of extracurricular activities. Admittedly, she was slightly less hot on the paperwork side of things, but, rightly or wrongly, I saw things holistically and forgave her for her shortcomings.

Then Annie's father passed away unexpectedly. Having lost my own father a while back, I tried to cut her some slack, but things went downhill. Book scrutinies were the most obvious indicator. Visiting classes with the chair of governors, Annie would hover by the classroom doorway, smiling charmingly but effectively blocking entry into the classroom. I knew something was not right, but I cut her some more slack, giving her a day's supply cover to catch up. She was grateful for my empathy, but things continued to slip and I became aware that other staff were beginning to talk. Why was Annie being allowed to get away with it? I felt very conflicted and quite uncomfortable with myself.

I eventually did have that conversation but had left it far too long and had damaged my credibility with other staff. I am sad to report too that Annie is no longer in teaching.

Time to reflect

Have you, as a leader, ever delayed having a conversation you knew you should have had?

How did you feel about yourself?

What was the eventual outcome?

Hannah Wilson, Executive Head of sibling schools Aureus School and Aureus Primary, puts it this way: 'Praise in public, criticise in private, but if you pussy-foot around it, people will talk about it. As leaders we are responsible for how people behave in the building, so if we allow rudeness, tardiness or a lack of ethics, we are effectively condoning their behaviour.'

Angela Browne is the Interim Deputy CEO of the Castle School Education Trust. She advises that the best way to prepare for having a difficult conversation is to articulate how you feel about having the conversation before you do it: 'It is easy to get into the bravado of "that person needs to be spoken to" or "that person needs to go" but when you are sitting in a room with them human to human, you sometimes question whether you have the right to judge, and remember, however bad you may be feeling, it will not be a patch on what they are going through.'

Angela says she finds it easier to prepare a list of the actions and behaviours that are causing concern. It depersonalises it and focuses you on the impact on the children, for example 'These are the things I have been seeing…', while providing the airtime to articulate what is going on.

Sometimes people will just be looking for a way out because the job has changed so much, and they cannot keep up. If this is the case, then it is a question of helping them to exit with dignity.

Ten tips for difficult conversations

1   Never act in the heat of the moment. Prepare what you want to say and then sleep on it but don't put things off.

2   State your purpose for having the conversation.

3   Reassure them that this is not disciplinary (unless it is of course!) and that you genuinely want to help them improve.

4   Tackle the behaviour and not the person. It should never come across as a personal attack.

5   State the facts. Remember, it is possible to speak the truth while still considering the other person's feelings. Avoid chucking in the kitchen sink, i.e. 'And another thing…'. Be clear and specific.

6   Set expectations for improvement.

7   Ask them whether they are willing to work towards those goals. (Largely rhetorical but you want them to work with you in willingness.) Also consider whether their willingness seems genuine or based on fear.

8   Ask what support they might need.

9   Agree next steps and timescales so that there can be no misunderstandings.

10   Keep a record of what has been agreed.

Of course, there will always be those more 'toxic' members of staff you will encounter – those saboteurs who, for a variety of reasons, may wish to derail your improvement ambitions. For advice on how to deal with such individuals, please see Chapter 6 of my book *Leading from the Edge*: 'The enemy within'.

Summary

- Successful leaders have the ability to foster good relationships and enable their team to achieve extraordinary things.
- The two greatest enablers of relationship-building are authenticity and positivity.
- Staff need to be able to align your actions as a leader with your stated values.
- High levels of positivity combined with low levels of authenticity indicate weak leadership.
- Low positivity + low authenticity = no followers.
- Effective leaders seldom have the monopoly on good ideas but encourage others to share theirs.
- Staff are more likely to stay in working environments where they feel valued, recognised and listened to.
- A good leader is not a hero but a hero-maker.
- Without a degree of risk-taking as a leader, you risk predictability, complacency and stagnation.
- Praise in public. Criticise in private.

3 Communication

You can have brilliant ideas, but if you can't get them across, your ideas won't get you anywhere.

Lee Lacocca

It is, I am afraid, an inevitable fact that you are never entirely going to win as school leader. In staff eyes, we are often damned if we do and damned if we don't. For example, my second headship was in a primary school that grew from 14 classes to 28 during my ten-year tenure. This was as a result of a massive housing expansion in the area. Inevitably, as the number of classrooms and playgrounds (there were six when I left) increased, I became less visible to staff. There are only so many places you can be at one time! I know that it troubled some of the longer-serving members of staff who could remember the days of it being a small village primary school. But on the weeks when my diary was a little freer and I got to spend more time in classrooms, people would sometimes grumble that I was checking up on them. You see you really can't win, and I did come to realise that it was unrealistic to expect people to understand the pressures of my role when they have never done it. In quite the same way, nobody understands what it is like to be a classroom teacher if they have never been one.

However, there is one thing in leadership that you really *do* have to get right, and that is the art of good communication.

Good communication is critical to being able to function as an effective leader. Most classroom teachers are skilled communicators, but they are generally used to communicating ideas to up to 30 pupils at a time. While school leaders may build on those skills, it is rather different. You often have to be able to think quickly and clearly, expressing both ideas and information to a wide range of audiences including pupils, staff, governors and the wider community. It is not necessarily about using the right vocabulary, grammar, and so on (although I am not diminishing their importance); I have met with and worked for some great school leaders and, although they may have very different personality traits and passions, they have all been exceptionally good communicators. They will talk to you about their beliefs and ideas about education, but anyone can do that. The difference is that they talk to you in a way that reaches out to your emotions and your own aspirations. They understand that their message needs to resonate deeply with their audience, because unless it does, it will not truly be understood, let alone supported. School leaders will spend most of each and every day in some kind of interpersonal interaction. Some do it so well and others perhaps less so. The difference those communication skills make has a wide impact on both the buy-in of all stakeholders and, ultimately, the effectiveness of the school. Few school leaders have received much in the way of communication training and this is a pity, I feel, because poor communication can lead to so many misunderstandings. Most of us have to learn on the job as we go along.

One of the most critical challenges you face early on as a school leader is to decide what your vision is for your team, department or school. Having decided that, equally critical is how you then communicate that vision to all stakeholders in a way that they can buy into.

I recently met up with **Hannah Wilson**. Hannah is the co-founder of #WomenEd as well as being the Executive Headteacher of Aureus School and Aureus Primary School in Didcot in Oxfordshire. Both were start-up schools serving a large, new housing estate of 30,500 new homes. At the time of my visit, Aureus School (secondary) was in its second year and had both Year 7 and Year 8 pupils. Aureus Primary was in its first year and only had pupils up to Year 2. Many of the classrooms in these dramatic, new-build schools remain empty but, as the schools grow organically year by year, they will eventually provide all-through education to the children in the area.

To start up once would be a daunting prospect but to start up twice in the space of two years is a feat of some magnitude. There are many logistical challenges. For example, I thought that *I* had spent a lot of time interviewing as the head of a large primary school, but Hannah once interviewed six people a day for three weeks, and on top of this you then have the induction of the new staff for these sibling schools.

So, how do you create and communicate the vision when everything and everyone is new?

Like me, Hannah is something of a fan of the literary work of Simon Sinek and, in particular, his book *Start With Why*. I talked a little bit about him in my chapter 'A sense of purpose' in *Ten Traits of Resilience*. While he doesn't write specifically about education, what he writes is very translatable to many schools of today. Imagine an archery target with three rings. 'What we do' is the outside ring, 'How we do it' is the middle ring and 'Why we do it' is the bullseye. Many organisations get lost in the 'What' and the 'How', so they lose sight of the bullseye 'Why'. Successful organisations know clearly what their 'Why' is and underline the 'What' and 'How' to stay true to that vision.

Although there are clearly many challenges in opening start-up schools, it also provided Hannah with a blank canvas and an opportunity to start with 'Why' and establish early on 'Who they are'. Clarity from the get-go. With Aureus School, the deputy headteachers were appointed early on and, as a senior leadership team, they were committed to doing things differently. Starting with an initial one-year group of Year 7s, how could they do this a different way in order to get them to where they need to be at the end of their education?

The school is black and white about what they are and what their DNA is. They talk about their 'Why', their values and their ethos at the start of each year. They are collaborative and outward-looking, seeking best practice rather than competition. They have taken lots of small contentious decisions, which, on their own, may not seem particularly significant but together create a different and distinctive ethos.

As is often the case, parents are attracted to schools with shiny new buildings full of chrome and glass. When talking to parents, Hannah tells them to ignore the glittering new build.

'If you want sets, that's not us. If you want homework detentions, it's not for you.'

We are Marmite. I like Marmite.

Hannah Wilson

Every great leader that I can think of has always had a vision. Nelson Mandela, for example, dreamed of a South Africa without apartheid. Henry Ford dreamed of making the automobile affordable for every man and woman. Lech Wałęsa dreamed of a Poland run by the workers to serve the common people. Whatever your leadership role or school situation, you will no doubt have ideas about how you would like to change things. These ideas fuel your vision and vision is so important because nothing of value happens unless it happens in someone's mind first.

What is vision?

Put quite simply, your vision is your big picture of how things ought to be in your school. If you like, it can be compared to a billboard image that shows others and reminds you of what it is you are working towards. Few of us will go about our day-to-day life in school without considering ways in which things could be improved. Perhaps reading standards are not as high as you would like, or behaviour or mental wellbeing of pupils are issues. When leaders start to put together those pieces, that vision starts to become clearer. Your billboard is a picture of your ideal school. As a teacher I can remember many times getting children to design posters on a variety of topics. I always told them that their poster should be colourful, attractive and convey their ideas simply, accurately and quickly. That is exactly what billboards do and exactly what your leadership vision should also do.

Don't be afraid to dream big. You can always temper things to meet the reality of the situation but starting with a vision allows you to consider ideas that may seem a little unlikely, but are, in fact, still possible. Value your instincts. If an idea excites you, the chances are that, if sold well, it will excite others too. If you want a good example of what can be achieved, against the odds, you would do well to take a read of my good friend Richard Gerver's (2014) book *Creating Tomorrow's Schools Today*. Richard turned around a failing primary school into one of international renown for innovation, by asking the simple question 'Why shouldn't schools be a little more like Disneyland?'

OK, this next exercise is a bit arty for me, but bear with me…

Time to reflect

Imagine your leadership vision as a billboard poster.

- What would it look like as an image?

- What would it say on it?

- How would you want people to react when they saw it?

- Now, if you're feeling very creative, have a go at designing it in the
  box below.

Once you have some clarity about what your vision is, you need to a) communicate it to other people and b) use it to lead them.

Communicating your vision to other people

It seems obvious to say that you need to communicate your vision to other people, but why? The answer is because, as we have established, you are not going to achieve anything without people following you and they are not going to follow you unless they trust you and, importantly, they know the direction that you are heading in.

Patrick Ottley-O'Connor would summarise the process of communicating a vision effectively as:

1 enthuse and **energise**

2 engage

3 empower.

First, you need to **enthuse** and **energise** people. If your vision is powerful enough, appealing enough and resonates with people, they will rise to the level and they will join you and throw their weight, enthusiasm and expertise behind you to help you achieve your goals.

However, it is almost inevitable that this will not get 100 per cent buy-in, for all manner of reasons. Some people may feel threatened, perhaps because they know they don't have the skills required for this new change of direction. We have talked already about the importance of those difficult conversations, but it is important to unpick why people may be rebelling against the vision. Consider the importance of confidence-building (reassuring them that they do have the capacity) and training needs (to plug the gaps in their skillset). There will, more than likely, be those who simply don't like the direction of travel on a philosophical level and choose to leave.

> I can remember, at the end of my first year of my second headship, I had several members of staff who moved on. It was a large staff and so some natural turnover was to be expected, but it was more than that. Everyone was terribly polite about it, no one actually said that they disagreed with the road we were travelling. There were no histrionics but, I suspect, the school was changing and it simply wasn't for them anymore. I can remember feeling slightly deflated about it at the time but, looking back, it was the right thing for all concerned. However strong your vision may be, it will not appeal to everyone. Don't beat yourself up about it.

No matter what our attempts to inform, it is our ability to inspire that will turn the tides.

Jan Phillips

Sharing a vision is central to the role of a school leader. It actually defines the difference between a person who leads people and one who simply manages them. The best leaders are outward-looking and collaborative. They see the wider educational landscape and draw on best practice to improve their own setting. Sharing a vision helps to give people the bigger picture of what things could be like. Done well, it helps to raise hopes and expectations. It inspires people and when people are inspired, they are far more likely to commit their time and energy to work on something.

You need to be communicating your vision all the time – not only by the things you say, but through your actions. You need to embody that vision because if your actions are in conflict then people will either fail to buy in, or they will soon lose faith.

Getting feedback

Engage people. Talk to your staff regularly. Tell them what you are thinking. Paint the big picture that you want them to see. Then sit back and listen, really listen, to what they have to say. Find out whether they are interested in your big picture and find out whether they have concerns. That is quite a brave thing to do but ignoring concerns is like wallpapering over the cracks. It may cover them up for now but they will surely reappear if you don't acknowledge them. If you have one or two concerns yourself, consider sharing them. In my experience, people tend to have more faith in a leader who displays a little humanity than one who displays a blind and dogmatic optimism.

Another good reason for getting feedback is that the more you talk and, importantly, *listen* to other people, the clearer your vision is likely to become. Whenever I applied for a teaching position, I would practise verbalising the answers to likely interview questions to anyone who would listen (even if they knew nothing about teaching, e.g. my dog). The process of hearing my thoughts **out loud** helped me to be clearer in articulating the points that I wanted to make. Talking with other people about your vision has much the same effect.

Talking to other people, you will get a clearer idea of how strong your vision really is. Not everybody will necessarily agree with your vision but if people get excited and animated when talking with you then you are probably onto a good thing.

Be prepared for the possibility that, having listened to feedback on your ideas, your vision may change somewhat as you may want to incorporate some of their thinking in with your own. This does not make your vision weak or faulty; it is just that other people's ideas will often make your vision stronger.

The devil is in the detail

After you have tested out (and possibly reshaped) your vision for your team, department or school, you need to work on the details. While this should not be rushed, it needs to be done at some pace, as it is only human nature that staff will want to know how this will impact them on a day-to-day basis. In particular, they will want to know whether it is going to mean more work! Making room for one new initiative might well mean having to do away with another.

My friend Neil used to work for BT and I can remember him once using a mail train as an analogy for innovation overload. You can only push so many sacks of mail in through the side doors before something has to be pushed out of the back.

Patrick Ottley-O'Connor refers to leaders as being 'barrier removal operatives'. It is their job to free staff from bureaucratic tasks that often have little or no impact, leaving teachers liberated to teach.

Simply piling on more work is not going to endear you to anyone and is likely to sink your ship before it even leaves port. It needs careful thought. Teacher wellbeing needs to be central to your plans if they are to succeed. You don't have to have all the answers in fine detail but you need some specifics available on how things would change and a clear, staged plan of how you are going to get from where you are now to where you want to be. Without this, people may come to view the big picture as fantasy art. The better the plan, the more likely it is that staff will see your vision (and you!) as credible and be willing to follow your lead. You may need to consider who else needs to be involved in that plan.

Anyone who ever worked in the senior leadership teams of either of the schools where I was head would tell you that I am an 'ideas' person. I am creative, but quite scatty – not exactly a doer-finisher! Fortunately, there were other members of the senior leadership team who were. They had a voracious appetite for work and a fine eye for detail, without which many of my ideas would never have come to fruition.

Whatever your personality type, you need to involve people with complementary skills to make it as good a plan as it can be.

If you want to go fast, go alone. If you want to go far, go together.

African proverb

Your job as a leader is now to help people take the vision and **empower** them to make it their own. By listening to the ideas of others and modifying the vision without compromising its core values, this becomes easier to do. Staff need a sense of ownership to be committed to the vision and they need to understand how their role fits in. By staff, I mean *all* staff: teachers, teaching assistants, midday supervisors, and site and office staff. They all need to know the importance of their contribution and how they fit into your big picture. More on this later in the book.

Staff (and governors too!) don't need to agree with every detail of your vision in order to follow you. They will, in all probability, have different ideas about how to make the vision work. This is fine and normal, and actually some of those ideas may enhance the vision. Richard Gerver talks about the difference between organisations that run with a working environment where there is an 'Assumption of Incompetence', where staff are micromanaged to deliver as efficiently as possible, which is terribly demoralising for staff, and those that empower people with an atmosphere of 'Assumed Excellence' (from a speech at London Business Forum, April 2019). There will always be one or two underperformance issues but, by and large, your people know their jobs, and very few people roll up to work with the intention of doing a bad job. Listen to them. **Jonny Mitchell** talked about the importance of people feeling that they could communicate with leaders as well as being communicated to. **Hannah Wilson** echoed these thoughts, talking about the notion of 'fierce conversations' and that in some schools such conversations only happen downwards. Staff need to feel **empowered** to talk to leaders about what they are unhappy about. People need to feel that they have your ear – not just being listened to, but actually *heard*. It is crucial to staff mental wellbeing and to **empowerment**.

Inevitably some people might engage with your vision more quickly than others. We are all in different places in our lives, both personally and professionally. School leaders are able to communicate parts of the vision that people can relate to. Some may struggle with the blue sky thinking of what the school might look like in five years' time. They can only see within the four walls of their classroom. It does not make them bad people; it is just where they are at this moment in time. That having been said, we sometimes have to say things that some people will not be quite ready to hear. Some will need time to think about new ideas before they are able to make sense of them, but it is important to introduce new ideas even if they are met with initial resistance from some. Some of the strongest and best ideas will meet with resistance but it does not make them any less worth striving for.

Leaders should be communicating the vision all the time. Staff will be looking to you for inspiration and to help keep them on the right track. The greater your enthusiasm and clarity of purpose, the more likely it is that staff will follow your lead.

Adapting your communication style over time

It is not so much about the act of communication but about how you do it. Most school leaders will not experience a start-up school situation such as that at Aureus School (see page 44). For many, starting new in post will involve changing systems and attitudes that already exist. You must be prepared for the fact that your communication style will need to change over time. Jonny Mitchell referred to how, when he started his headship, he was very clear about what he wanted and there was no wiggle room in this. It was a case of 'This is what we stand for…'. Jonny was less accepting of feedback earlier on but, having established values and vision, he has been able to become more collaborative. Different schools require different approaches, so what has worked for you in one school may not serve you as well in another. It is about finding out how to get the best out of people.

This is also reflected in Patrick's experiences. He has to go in with a vision and get people to help. His communication style is pace-setting and directive, establishing non-negotiables, such as no mobile phones in school. Bearing in mind that Patrick works as an interim head, generally staying only one year in a particular setting, he has to move at pace. Having established the vision and the non-negotiables, he aims to move towards a more affiliative, coaching style by half term, listening to people, removing barriers to teaching, such as four-page lesson plans, but ultimately still making the decisions, because, as he says, 'That's what I am paid to do.'

Ten tips for communication

1 **Get to know your staff, what interests them and what motivates them.** While you need to be consistent in your message, how you deliver it may vary according to the personalities involved, so adapt your delivery to get the best out of everyone. One-to-ones are good for this.

2 **Be aware of the unconscious signals your body language gives off.** I used to tell infants practising for the school nativity that when it came to the actual performance and the hall was full of parents, there would always be at least one person in the audience looking at them at any one time, so if they fidgeted or put their finger up their nose, someone was bound to see. Similarly, as you walk around school, there will always be someone watching you and, consciously or unconsciously, drawing conclusions about your mood or state depending not only on the expression on your face, but also on your tone of voice, the way you walk or the way you hold yourself. There is definitely a place for showing a little vulnerability and I am not suggesting you walk around with a smile permanently plastered on your face. Rather than follow you, they will try to have you carted away, but they are watching you. Just saying!

3 **Speak truthfully at all times.** Trying to be a crowd pleaser or bending the truth will rarely do you good in the long term. In order to truly know what is happening on the ground, you need people to feel they are able to open up to you. In order to do this, they need to feel that they can trust you. Trust is hard won and easily lost. Tell it as it is while being aware of the feelings of your audience.

4 **Communicate often and clearly.** In the absence of clear information, people will fill in the gaps for themselves, often incorrectly. Don't

believe me? Try sending round a note saying 'Emergency staff meeting at 12.30 pm' and just watch the rumour mill spin into action. It is like lighting the blue touch paper and then standing well back. BOOM! You will probably only do it the once though.

5   **Limit the use of whole-school emails.** They may be convenient but are often, by their very nature, completely impersonal and thus lack impact. It is as though you are speaking *at* people rather than *to* them. Get personal and go out and have a conversation with them. If you lead a large staff, meet them in teams. It shows that you care and the more they think you care, the more likely they are to engage with what you have to say.

6   **Listen without interrupting.** I will hold my hands up and say I was not always good at this. There is a difference between actively listening as opposed to waiting for the other person to take a breath for you to interject! Listening should not be threatening if you are clear in your beliefs and the rationale behind them, and some of the best ideas are uncovered by sharing individual insights.

7   **Avoid using jargon, 'on trend' terminology and endless acronyms.** They seem to change on a yearly basis and actually mask the clarity of the message you are trying to deliver. It doesn't make you look more intelligent; in my humble view, it makes you look like you are trying to hide behind something. Enough said.

8   **Communicate using a wide variety of formats.** Communication with parents is increasingly through electronic forms. Schools are increasingly using social media as a communication tool. It is of course a double-edged sword. I have seen some vile content posted about schools and individuals on Facebook (usually from parents who would never dare to say such things to someone's face but think it is OK to do so in the virtual world of communication), but platforms such as Facebook, Twitter and LinkedIn can also be powerful tools in communicating with parents and the wider community. Hannah Wilson, for example, has never paid for an advert for staff for the Aureus schools. She is a skilled communicator and uses social media to great effect.

9   **Check your ego and replace it with empathy.** I think all leaders have something of an ego. I think you have to have a bit of one to put yourself out there in the first place. When honest messages

are delivered with empathy and care, good things start to happen. Empathetic leaders show a level of transparency and trust that is not communicated by those who display a carefully manufactured mask that hides a fragile ego.

10 **Know what you are talking about.** Sounds obvious I know. I studied drama at university and can remember an occasion when I was supposed to have read a play by the Swedish playwright August Strindberg to discuss in a seminar group the following day. I can't tell you the name of the play because I never actually read it. Too much playing pool in the Student Union bar the night before (I was not always the most diligent of students, I'm afraid). I thought I could wing it by reading the jacket notes and a cursory skim of the list of characters. Turns out I couldn't. Our tutor saw right through me in the first five minutes. The 'fake it till you make it' days are long gone, and slick patter will not replace a lack of substance. You need a good command of your subject matter, otherwise people will not give you the time of day.

The best communicators in my experience are very good at listening and make astute observations. They are able to communicate their thoughts effectively in both one-to-one and group situations. They do it by getting to know people. This gives them an advantage in knowing people's key motivators and enables them to 'read the room', sensing moods, dynamics and concerns of those they are talking to. They realise that it is not just the content of the message that counts but also how it is delivered. Given that you will spend much of your day communicating with people in some way, shape or form, the skills are worth working on.

Summary

- Good communication is critical to being able to function as an effective leader.
- New in post? Clarity is vital from the get-go. Be clear about what you stand for and what is in your DNA.
- Your vision is your big picture about what things ought to be like in your department or school.

Communication

- In order to sell your vision, you need to enthuse and energise your staff if they are to buy into it.
- Engage people. Tell them what you are thinking and where you want to go. Then… listen.
- Don't be afraid to adapt your vision in the light of feedback. It is not a sign of weakness but a sign of strength.
- Push some mailbags out of the back of the train before adding new ones.
- Avoid appointing a team 'in your likeness'. You need complementary strengths to make a good plan great.
- Your communication style needs to adapt as your department or school evolves.
- Speak truthfully at all times.

---

4 Know thyself (part 1): Introvert and extrovert leaders

Quiet people have the loudest minds.

Stephen Hawking

I first started teaching in a primary school over 30 years ago. In some ways it seems a lifetime ago and in others as if it were only yesterday. Those were very different times but among the people to make a big impression on me were the local headteachers. Two things particularly struck me about them. Firstly, there was a disproportionate number of men in the role given the overall gender balance within the primary sector. Secondly, they were all big personalities and for the most part I was in awe of them.

My own headteacher was absent throughout my NQT year as he was on secondment, studying peace in Northern Ireland (a secondment of that length and nature is something that is hard to imagine today). But when he finally did appear at the beginning of my second year, he made an immediate impression. He was a larger-than-life character who was an ex-RAF officer, wore a badged blazer, often with a cravat, smoked a pipe around school and appropriately enough drove a red Triumph Spitfire. He immediately took me under his wing and, on one occasion, having failed to be impressed when observing one of my creative writing lessons, demonstrated the importance of a visual stimulus by setting fire to my classroom wastepaper bin, setting off the fire alarm and causing the immediate evacuation of the whole school.

Then there was the female head down the road who had a reputation for a vicious temper with children and staff alike. She spent much of the time shut away in her office and when someone dared to knock upon her door she would bellow, 'GO AWAY!' Every now and then she would fling open her office door, only to disappear like a tornado down the corridor to who knows where. Nobody dared to ask.

Also in the locality was a husband and wife pair of heads who ran an infant and junior school on the same site and always left at lunchtime on a Friday to attend meetings. Everyone knew that they were driving to the coast to go sailing for the weekend. And finally, there was the head who 'went to a meeting' for the day but was spotted later that evening on the highlights of the golf on BBC Two.

These are just a few examples of the way leadership was modelled to me in my early career, so my perception was therefore that to be a school leader you needed to be a larger-than-life character who was extroverted and preferably had some kind of eccentricity that defined you to others: a little like each incarnation of Doctor Who – essentially the same character but with some costume quirks that define them, for example Tom Baker's scarf, Matt Smith's penchant for wearing a fez or Jodie Whittaker's short trousers and braces.

Were all heads these extroverted, outgoing characters? Weren't there any introverted heads around? Well, if there were, I honestly cannot recall them. It might be that, by their nature, they were not so 'in your face' and did not court the same kind of attention, but I suspect the vast majority were these big personalities. 'Why?' you ask. The answer is that headship was a very different role back in the '80s and early '90s.

Local Management of Schools was not introduced until the Education Reform Act of 1998, giving schools control over their budgets for the very first time. Prior to this, the only real budgets heads controlled were the school trip fund and the stationery budget, the latter of which was, in reality, organised by the school secretary. (Our school secretary used to jealously guard the stationery cupboard, keeping it locked at all times. You would have to grovel for a roll of sticky tape! All that changed when one enterprising member of the senior leadership team took the key from the drawer in her desk one lunchtime when she was out of school. He took it to the local locksmith and had several copies made, before returning the key unnoticed. Funnily enough, her termly stocktaking sessions never tallied up from that point on!)

Many schools in the '80s and early '90s had little control of their own staffing too. Our local authority would use a formula based upon pupil numbers to decide how many teachers there should be in the school and would recruit newly qualified teachers centrally, as part of a pool, to plug gaps. I was allocated to my first school. Neither they nor I had any say in the process as far as I am aware.

There were no teaching assistants back then either, so fewer overall staff – just teachers, secretary, caretakers, cleaners, the 'dinner ladies' (as they were called back then) and the cooks. (We had a brilliant Polish cook who saw it as her mission to fatten me up, because I was like a beanpole back then, and would give me double portions of chips every day. Her strategy eventually worked, but there was a time delay until I was about 45!)

There was no curriculum, as such. Children worked their way through textbooks for maths, grammar and handwriting, and teachers more or less followed their own particular interests for the other subjects, doing as much or as little of them as they chose. Some kids would endure topics on autumn year on year. Roger, who taught in the same year group as me, hated doing music so he just didn't do it. No one ever checked up. No one led on teaching and learning because it was basically a free-for-all.

So, I think I have established that schools were very different places back then and as such required a very different breed of leader. I use the term 'leader' rather loosely. There was not an awful lot of 'leading' going on to be honest – 'management' perhaps at best.

What schools required back in the '80s was a figurehead. They needed to be a pillar of the community who would represent the school at events such as the village fête. Someone to lead assembly and a rousing rendition of 'Autumn days when the grass is jewelled…'. They were also required to be a firm disciplinarian, someone who would scare the bejesus out of a child if ever they were sent to stand outside their office. Someone whom even the parents were in awe of and would not dare answer back. And so, it took a certain kind of character to fulfil that kind of a role. Shy and retiring would not really fit the bill. I am not being critical of such leaders; they were very much of their time and I'm sure that if anybody was to look back on my 15 years of headship in, say, 2050, they would regard it with much the same raised eyebrow as I cast my eye over school leadership in the 1980s.

Then there was the process of how people got leadership roles back then. It was often a case of not what you knew but who you knew, and to get yourself known you had to put yourself out there and create an impression.

In my second year of teaching I signed up to almost every after-school course (and there were courses almost nightly at staff development centres across the county) run by one particular senior adviser (we will call him Sean), specifically because I wanted to be noticed and I knew that Sean carried a lot of influence. It certainly worked because I got my first senior leadership role after three years. (Far too early, looking back – I knew nothing!) It was a primary school in the shadow of an enormous red-brick, Victorian mill. The school was on Rosemary's patch. Rosemary was a senior adviser with a fearsome reputation. She had an old-fashioned card file box in which she had a card with notes on every teacher on her patch. I must have made a good impression on her because she sent a very experienced teacher from another school who was clearly on her 'naughty step' to observe me teach. I had been noticed, and after only four terms I was seconded as acting deputy head to a nearby school. I went on to get the substantive position and eight years later, when my head retired, I took over.

Without having made that first impression, my career could have turned out very differently. You really did have to put yourself out there in order to be noticed and that is probably more comfortable for someone who is an extrovert than an introvert. And so, I think it starts to become clear why so many outgoing characters rose to the top. A myth was perpetuated: that in order to be a school leader, you needed to be an extrovert.

Nowadays schools require a very different kind of a leader: someone who can, well, lead! Someone who can inspire and motivate. Someone with excellent communication and interpersonal skills. Someone who can lead and talk with authority on teaching and learning. Someone with a sound understanding of financial planning and human resources. Someone who will stand up for what they know to be right and hold their nerve under pressure. Someone who can work well in a world of subtlety and nuance. A rather different kind of school leader and that changes things dramatically.

What is an extrovert?

Extroverts tend to find their energy interacting with other people and are often very sociable, making friends easily. They present themselves in much the same way in public and in private. They often think out loud and are vocal and outspoken in a group situation. They tend to make decisions quickly and are easily distracted. They learn by doing. Extroverts tend to unload their thinking and emotions as they go along. They are happy to wing it when needed and are happy to talk about their accomplishments.

What is an introvert?

Introverts find their energy from inside themselves. They may well have a smaller circle of friends, but these are people they are very close to. Introverts often have a public and a private self, which they move between depending on the situation. They are often quiet in large groups and will sometimes mentally rehearse what they want to say before talking. They prefer to take their time in making decisions and can concentrate for long periods without being distracted. They often learn by observation. Introverts have a tendency to bottle up their emotions. They need time to prepare and are often very humble about their accomplishments.

A common misapprehension is that introversion equals shyness. Not so. Shyness is caused by social psychological anxiety, says Kahnweiler (2018), and can, in extreme cases, be quite debilitating. There may be some overlap between introversion and shyness, but introversion is more about how the brain is wired up. As such, it is not a fault, flaw or something to be overcome.

Extroverts really crave large amounts of stimulation, whereas introverts feel at their most alive and their most switched-on and their most capable when they're in quieter, more low-key environments.

Susan Cain (2012)

Do watch Susan Cain's TED Talk if you get the chance (it's available at www.ted.com/talks/susan_cain_the_power_of_introverts). It will make you think very differently about introverts and extroverts and particularly what we unwittingly put some introverted pupils through in terms of teaching style and class organisation.

When I am running courses on stress management, I often give participants a personality test in the form of a quiz. It always seems to go down well (it appears everybody loves a quiz!). The test asks people to pick which of two opposite statements best reflects their personality. Have a go.

Do you have a 'type A' or 'type B' personality?

Tick the boxes that most apply to you.

Type A	Type B
☐ I hold feelings in.	☐ I freely express feelings.
☐ I am competitive.	☐ I am not competitive.
☐ I am impatient when waiting.	☐ I can wait calmly.
☐ I am a perfectionist.	☐ I can live with something not being quite perfect.
☐ I tend to work on several things at once without completing them.	☐ I tend to work on one thing at once.
☐ I tend to rush tasks.	☐ I tend to take time over tasks.
☐ I usually take work home.	☐ I rarely take work home.
☐ I tend to talk quickly.	☐ I have slow, measured speech.
☐ I tend to interrupt conversations and finish other people's sentences.	☐ I can listen and let another person finish their sentences.
☐ I arrive at appointments late or just in time.	☐ I arrive at appointments with time to spare.
☐ I have a limited social life and limited interests.	☐ I have a good social life and a variety of interests.
☐ I am generally dissatisfied with work.	☐ I am generally satisfied with work.
☐ I am generally dissatisfied with life.	☐ I am generally satisfied with life.

So, are you more of a 'type A' or 'type B' person?

As I am sure you have guessed, type A personalities are more prone to stress. People taking the test rarely identify as being completely type A or type B, but most people skew to either A or B. And so it is with introversion and extroversion.

Personally, I am a mixture. I skew towards extroversion. You have to be something of an extrovert to stand up as a keynote speaker in front of several hundred people. For sure, I still get very nervous beforehand, sometimes to the point of nausea, but when it goes well (and if you are considering me to speak at an event, it absolutely *always* goes well – never a slip-up!) and I have established a good rapport with the audience, I really do thrive on it. So that is the extrovert in me. On the other hand, thrust me into a room of complete strangers and tell me to work the room? That is my worst nightmare. I become very quiet and feel socially awkward.

I also think I have changed a lot over time. In my second headship, I spent my days surrounded by 800 children and around 100 staff, but these days, if I am not away speaking, I am often writing and will spend much of the day on my own with Eddie, my good-natured, but extremely stubborn, golden retriever, my companion. Do not get me wrong; I love what I do, but it is a real contrast to working in a school and I think it has amplified the more introverted side of my nature.

Some people argue that there is a third type of personality, that of ambivert, sharing characteristics of both extroverts and introverts – acting like an extrovert in social situations and an introvert when on your own, effectively sliding up and down on a spectrum according to the situation. I certainly know of headteachers who, by the public nature of their role, are quite extroverted in their behaviour but become quite hermit-like at the weekends and holidays as they seek the isolation, needing to recharge their batteries ready for the new term or the week ahead.

Time to reflect

Would you identify yourself as skewed to introversion or extroversion?

Do you present as the same person in public as in private?

What situations make you feel uncomfortable professionally?

What situations make you feel uncomfortable socially?

Do you need time on your own to 'recharge your batteries' after spending time with people?

Know thyself (part 1)

The real clincher is the last question. Jennifer B. Kahnweiler PhD (2015), a global speaker and 'champion for introverts', suggests that if your answer to that question is categorically YES, it is more than likely that you are quite introverted, but if it is more of a medium sort of a YES, then you are probably more of an extrovert.

It is estimated that somewhere between a third and half the world's population skew towards introversion and yet in the world of business over 90 per cent of high-level executives identify themselves as extroverts and 65 per cent of executives view introversion as an obstacle to leadership. And yet there are some very successful introverted leaders. It is somewhat ironic that Mark Zuckerberg, the founder of arguably the greatest social network site Facebook, is famously shy and introverted. Susan Cain (2013), author of *Quiet: The Power of Introverts in a World That Can't Stop Talking*, says that Bill Gates, the founder of Microsoft, is also an introvert.

An example of an introverted British leader is Vikas Shah, the CEO of textile and commodities business Swisscot Group. Shah was awarded an MBE for services to business and the economy. When faced with situations that might be challenging, for instance networking events, he will plan his exit strategy, mingling at the start, perhaps listening to a speaker and then excusing himself. He does not feel the pressure to be the last man or woman standing.

And then there is Barack Obama. In an article in *The New York Times Magazine* on 12 October 2010, entitled 'Education of a president', Peter Baker noted that Obama's aides 'have learned that it can be good if he has a few moments after a big East Room event so he can gather his energy again'. Sharing his daily routines with *The New York Times*, the former president would have dinner at 6.30 pm when in the White House with his wife and daughters and then withdraw to his private office along the hall from his bedroom. Here he would regularly spend four to five hours largely by himself. Sounds like introvert behaviour to me.

Certainly, Obama is more of an introvert than his successor, who seems to tweet instant reactions to anything that even mildly annoys him. I certainly know who I would rather have with their finger on the nuclear trigger! That's enough of the politics. Move on, James.

So, I think we have established that while introverted leaders may be under-represented, they nonetheless can be very successful in politics and in business, and I see absolutely no reason why this should not be the case in schools.

Angela Browne says that there is sometimes a misunderstanding of the set of functions around modern school leadership. Stripped right back it is about:

1   communication
2   getting people on board.

When you think about it like that, you do not need to be a huge personality, like the heads of 30 years ago, to deliver on leadership.

There is a perception that heads have to be a certain way in order to succeed. We do ourselves a huge disservice by not taking into account the diversity of leadership styles.

Angela Browne

That having been said, there are challenges for the introverted school leader. But we all have our challenges!

Challenges facing the introverted school leader

Firstly, you have to be prepared to step outside your comfort zone. Like it or not, communicating to groups of varying sizes and composition is part of the leadership role. I really don't think I have come across a leader who is not comfortable leading an assembly. It is, after all, an extension of class teaching, our bread and butter. (I used to relish assemblies. It was my opportunity, in a day often full of admin, to actually spend time with the children. Others may enjoy it less than me, but still be quite comfortable doing it.) However, talking to a hall full of parents at an induction evening may be a very different thing if you are naturally introverted. You need to become comfortable with it or at least masquerade that you are comfortable with it, and that only comes with practice.

My friend Steve developed an anxiety issue driving up steep hills. It came seemingly out of nowhere. He would glaze over, and his palms would become sweaty, making gripping the wheel an issue, which in turn contributed to his sense of feeling out of control. As a result, he started planning routes to avoid roads that he knew had steep hills. It became a huge issue for him. He saw his GP and was referred for cognitive behaviour therapy. The therapist told him that avoiding hills was just making things worse. It brought him temporary relief but, as he was encountering hills less often, it became much more of an event when he did. The treatment was to go out for 'driving practice' a couple of times a week, gradually building up to steeper and steeper hills until he had built his confidence back up.

Comfort zones grow when we step outside them, but remain inside them and they start to shrink.

So, what are some of the other challenges facing an introverted school leader? Jennifer Kahnweiler (2018) identifies six challenges affecting introverted leaders. Allow me to extrapolate these and see how they may apply to school leadership.

1. People exhaustion

This is not to suggest that introverted leaders are anti-social and they may well enjoy their interactions with other people up to a point. They have a lot of inward energy, but limited reserves of the outward energy needed to interact with others. As leader you need to connect with others, but it does deplete your reserves and in a school environment you could be interacting with dozens, if not hundreds, of people each and every day. How much you 'have in the tank' will vary not only from person to person but at different times. High volumes of interactions will deplete the introverted school leader's tank more quickly. As Angela Browne has said, 'The key is to know yourself and structure in times of introversion in order to prepare for something big.'

For the extroverted leaders among you, Kahnweiler encourages you to force a smile, baring your teeth and holding it for ten seconds. That may seem very false and uncomfortable but is akin to what introverted leaders go through many times a day at work.

2. Pace of change

Thirty years ago, there were only four channels on TV, and you could watch the news three times a day. Most people read a newspaper to find out what was going on in the world. As I write this, *Notting Hill* (the film) is 20 years old. Re-watch it. Early on in the film, Anna Scott, Julia Roberts' character, is forced to knock on the door of William Thacker (Hugh Grant), a humble bookshop owner, because she has had orange juice spilled down her top and needs to use a phone. Seems impossible to believe that she would not have had a mobile phone back then, nor that there would not have been any social media platforms with someone posting a picture of her on Twitter, Facebook, Instagram or Snapchat. (To be fair, I don't understand what Snapchat is; I am just mentioning it in the hope of sounding current!) My point is this: the pace of change in society is exponential and that is reflected in schools. Only five years ago, most schools were part of a local authority system that had existed for several decades largely unchanged, and few people would have heard of a multi-academy trust, for example. Change is accelerating, not slowing down, and I cannot foresee that changing any time soon. It is frenetic. In Ofsted terms, if a school goes into 'Requires improvement', you are expected to come up with a plan pretty damn smartish. Introverted leaders may perhaps find it hard to be in situations where they have to make speedy decisions, when they may not feel they have all the necessary information and would prefer to reflect on ideas and issues before reaching a conclusion.

3. Interruptions

I find it really hard to settle to tasks and, if I am being honest, I always have. The only reason this book ever got finished was because I had a deadline. It was the same with both of my other books. I am a butterfly, though not as pretty. It was somewhat true of my time as a head. Just an email arriving unexpectedly could be enough to blow me off course from what I wanted to get done that day, but more often than not, it would be a knock on the door from a member of staff or a call put through from the school office. This can be off-putting for anyone but if you need your inner space it can be particularly trying.

In meetings too, introverts will tend to appreciate the power of 'pause and breathe'. Unfortunately, extroverts tend to abhor a vacuum and tend to fill the void with their own thoughts, often being perceived as interrupting the flow of their more introvert-skewed colleague.

4. Pressure to self-promote

There is still a perception that in order to get on you have to sell yourself and I guess this is true up to a point. The savvy school leader will construct a letter of application, personal statement or CV that paints their achievements in a positive light. I never lied but I was not going to draw attention to our dip in Year 6 SATs results in maths in my application for my second headship! As such, applications tend to become 'Our greatest hits' compilations, rather than a list of our tracks that never made it into the charts. I think there is a general acceptance that this is how you have to play the game, but I think it is more comfortable territory for the extroverts among us than the introverts. A tendency towards humility and finding the whole idea of networking difficult can potentially prove a challenge for introverted school leaders.

5. An emphasis on teamwork

When we think of our ideal school, we often think of everybody getting along as 'one big happy team', thinking out loud, sharing ideas and bouncing off one another to create the best possible environment for children to learn. This inevitably requires a lot of interaction and this is not necessarily a natural or comfortable environment for the introvert. As a head, I like to think I knew my staff pretty well. I can remember a few years ago our chair of governors, well-meaningly but perhaps rather naively, asking to speak to representatives from each year group about ways of improving the school. I had nothing to hide and so agreed to it, allowing staff to choose their representatives. Bearing in mind that we were a four-form-entry primary school, there were plenty of people to choose from, but I was not in the least surprised when the most extroverted teachers from each year group put themselves forward and were chosen. It was a missed opportunity in my view, because there is no correlation between being the most vocal and having the best ideas. As leaders we need to think of ways of structuring meetings to get the best out of both our introverted and our extroverted staff.

6. The perception gap

When I am at the more introverted end of my spectrum (it is a scale that I slide up and down between introversion and extroversion depending on situation), I know other people find me difficult to read. I think my facial expression changes from my animated, very smiley, nodding persona with blinking, which means I am listening and engaged with you, and my rather blank face. This means one of two things: a) I am really thinking nothing at all (which believe me does happen a lot!) or b) I am processing what you are saying. I am aware that that this may come over as being bored or aloof, but this is not the image I mean to project. This is the perception gap. I have been giving keynote speeches at conferences for over six years now and I am always looking out into the audience trying to gauge their reaction. I am hoping that my message is getting through and trying to see whether my jokes are hitting the mark.

Again, if you are thinking of booking me, my messages always get through and my sense of humour is tasteful, well-timed and hysterical! In reality, there is always a very small minority of delegates who seem disengaged. I think how well you engage with my speaking and writing partly depends on where you are on your leadership journey, but there are always one or two who come up to me afterwards to talk, or contact me by email, to say that that they have really engaged with my messages. I had completely misread their facial expressions. They were not bored or uninterested at all. They were processing what I was saying. These, I suspect, were the more introverted leaders among the audience. I'm not an expert, but perhaps this is a challenge more introverted school leaders face; people can't always read you and that can lead to misunderstandings.

Overcoming challenges for the introverted school leader

So, while there are some challenges along the way for the introverted school leader, Kahnweiler (2018) suggests a four-step process for overcoming them. This can best be summarised as:

1. Preparation

This plays to the introverted school leader's strength. Try writing questions prior to a meeting or set aside time to research topics in advance. You will feel more in control and therefore more relaxed. If it is an appointment, get there early. I occasionally lecture on interview skills for Derby University and this is the advice I give students. Our bodies can only stay in a state of heightened anxiety for short periods so arriving early gives you time to acclimatise.

2. Presence

The better prepared you are, the less preoccupied you will be, and the more others will perceive you as engaged and 'in the room' and be able to read your thoughts.

3. Pushing yourself

You need to step outside your comfort zone. My first professional engagement as a speaker was speaking to around 60 sixth-form careers advice teachers at an event at Derby University. I only had to speak for ten minutes and I did not know how I was going to fill the time. I very nearly bottled it until **Peter Anderton** encouraged me to have a go and see it as a learning experience. It actually went quite well, and it gave me a foundation of confidence from which I could build. Introvert or extrovert, we all need to push those boundaries in order to feel more confident. Make sure you deliver your key messages early on in any meeting.

4. Practice

It takes around three weeks to embed new thinking so give yourself other opportunities, however small, to take yourself out of your comfort zone and practise the things that you feel least comfortable with. Trust me: they get better with practice.

The benefits and drawbacks of being an introverted or extroverted school leader

(These are my perceptions. Feel free to disagree.)

Extroverts: benefits	Introverts: benefits
• Can readily communicate with a wide variety of stakeholders. • Quick to form close associations with others. • Work well in group settings. • Highly sociable, preferring to spend the majority of time with other people. • Often very determined and likely to take charge in any given situation.	• Less dependent on encouragement from others. Self-reliant. • Cautious and deliberate. • Precise and detail-orientated. • Generally steady in mood. • Accommodating as a rule and good listeners.

And the drawbacks?

Extroverts: drawbacks	Introverts: drawbacks
• Can't always make emotionless, analytical judgements. • Can sometimes struggle to concentrate on what other people are saying. • May have a tendency to get lonely if not in the company of others. • May thrive too much on external validation. • May appear to others as too confident or even a bit cocky.	• May be uncomfortable in networking-type events. • Could be risk-averse. • Tendency to hold back and not express opinions in meetings. • Might be overly reliant on own resources, thus closed to the ideas of others. • Find it difficult to collaborate and work in group situations.

Of course, these pros and cons reflect my ideas about leaders who operate at either end of the spectrum between introversion and extroversion.

So, who makes the better leader?

Well, as we have established, times have changed and the myth that only extroverts make good leaders is exactly that: a myth.

In her March 2012 TED Talk, 'The Power of Introverts', Susan Cain suggests that introverted leaders may well achieve better outcomes than their extroverted counterparts, particularly if they are leading proactive employees, as they are more likely to let people run with their own ideas, whereas highly extrovert leaders often put their own stamp on things, unwittingly suppressing the ideas of others, which may, in reality, be better.

I do wonder whether extrovert teams are best led by an introverted leader and vice versa. A study by Adam M. Grant, Francesca Gino and David A. Hofmann, published online in the *Academy of Management Journal* in 2011, suggests that this may be the case. Their studies into the productivity of pizza stores showed that stores with leaders with a high rate of extroversion achieved higher profits when matched with staff who were passive, but that the effects were reversed when they were matched with more proactive staff. They put this down to extroverted leaders being less receptive to the proactivity of others.

The reality is that you are unlikely to discover many school teams where the leader is an extrovert and everyone else is an introvert and vice versa, plus most of us live on some kind of spectrum, shifting to a degree depending on situation and circumstances. Teams of staff will be made up of a wide range of personalities and preferred working styles.

How to lead the differing personality types

Introverted staff

- Send out agendas before meetings with a clarity of purpose so that they have a chance to think things through beforehand and decide what they would like to contribute and say. (Besides, nobody likes a meeting with no real purpose and, believe me, I have sat through a few of those in my time – I probably led one or two on a bad day!)
- Concentrate on one issue at a time.
- Avoid noisy brainstorming sessions, allowing staff break-out spaces to consider the points under discussion. Don't demand instant answers of them.
- Give them time warnings for whatever you want them to finish doing.
- Avoid interrupting them.

Extroverted staff

- Avoid structuring meetings so tightly that they feel constrained.
- Provide them with opportunities to talk things out by providing optional brainstorming sessions.
- Let them dive right into a project and accept that they may well be busy when you want to talk to them.
- Publicly compliment and encourage their enthusiasm.
- Give them opportunities to shine. My first deputy head, Richard Gerver, and I were both pretty extroverted and one of the reasons that our partnership worked so well was that we both knew when to stand back and let the other have their place in the spotlight.

Opposite leaders

Let's focus this down a little and concentrate on you and your fellow leaders. Where the magic truly happens in schools is in the power of opposites. A chemistry of people who accept that they have their differences but that those differences, used in collaboration towards a shared vision, make them more than the sum of their parts. Lofty words, I know, and sometimes hard to achieve (goodness only knows, I have worked with some people who have driven me nuts and I am sure I did them!), but the commitment to making those relationships work is the game-changer.

Their relationships are the most successful when they stop focusing on their differences and use approaches that move them forward toward results.

Jennifer B. Kahnweiler (2015)

Ten tips for working with other leaders with contrasting personality types

1 Accepting your differences actually builds empathy, which will help any partnership.
2 Accept that in times of stress, extroverts will probably want to talk about it whereas introverts may well need space.

3   Take time to do some reading on personality styles and what other leaders around you may need.

4   Accept the fact that you are never going to change them.

5   Talk about your differences, thus removing the elephant in the room.

6   Accept that there will be battles and, provided they happen behind closed doors, they may ultimately be to the benefit of the school. You may reach a better solution.

7   Don't lose sight of your shared vision.

8   Walk together, talk together.

9   Match tasks to your personality types, with clear responsibilities.

10 Share the credit.

Operating as an ambivert

To get the best out of your team of staff, you have to adapt your style, just as you do when teaching a class full of children.

I suspect that whichever direction we are naturally skewed towards, most school leaders operate as ambiverts, incorporating aspects of both leadership styles depending partly on mood and partly on circumstances. They draw upon both their inner extrovert and introvert in order to lead others to work at their best.

Ambiverts:

- Enjoy being with other people, but they do need a break from them in order to recharge their batteries.

- Are talkative when interested in a subject but will be happy at times to sit back and take it all in.

- Are adventurous and like to try new things but equally they do like time to prepare.

- Feed off the buzz of school life, particularly when things are going well, but they can also be easily discouraged.

- Enjoy discourse and often think out loud but there are times when they grow weary of the opinions of others.

So, what kind of a leader are you? There is no one right way to do the job. The key to any leadership success is achieving balance.

Summary

- Modern school leaders are required to carry out a wide variety of roles beyond that of the historical, figurehead approach.

- Leadership today requires subtlety and nuance, calling for a different kind of leader.

- Extroverted leaders require high levels of stimulation.

- Introverted leaders feel the most switched on and capable in quieter environments but recognise the need to 'put themselves out there'.

- Whatever the stereotypes, introverted leaders can, and do, make good heads!

- Extroverted and introverted leaders are rarely polarised.

- Many leaders exist as ambiverts, displaying traits of both depending on the situation.

- Regardless of personality type, school leadership is essentially about a) communication and b) getting people on board.

- Remember the four **P**s: **P**reparation, **P**resence, **P**ush yourself, **P**ractice.

- The people you lead are also skewed either to introversion or extroversion. Adapt your style. One size does not fit all here.

- There is no one right way to be a school leader – the best leaders achieve balance.

5 Know thyself (part 2): Playing to your strengths

Don't try to be anyone else. Don't try to emulate what someone is doing. Play to your strengths.

Anjelah Johnson

Please would you bear with me a minute and complete the exercise on the following page.

Once you've completed the activity, be honest with yourself: which of the boxes did you find the easiest to complete? When I think about many of the leaders I have interviewed over the last five years, they have found the weaknesses box easier to complete than the strengths. A large number eventually completed the strengths box but it took them longer to fill in than their weaknesses. It has not greatly surprised me. After five years of reflection and three books later, I still find it easier to identify some of my weaknesses as a school leader. So, to be clear, I was no 'super-head', just a good head (I like to think) working in a school with very challenging circumstances set against a background of very rapid growth.

Time to reflect

List your five greatest failings as a school leader.

1.

2.

3.

4.

5.

Now list for me your five greatest strengths as a school leader.

1.

2.

3.

4.

5.

When I think back to my own career as a school leader, my **weaknesses** included:

- **A tendency to take negative feedback as personal criticism** when that was not always the intention. As such I would sometimes leap to the defensive.

- **Poor time-management skills at times.** Like everyone else, I would have a long 'to-do' list but would often target the easiest, quickest actions in an effort to tick things off rather than tackle the bigger issues that would have the most impact.

- **Sometimes I over-delegated** in order to keep on top of my own workload. It was a difficult balance to get. Most staff wanted any discipline issues to be dealt with by the head, but as I had over 800 primary-aged pupils, this was not always practicable. Nonetheless, I sometimes took my eye off the ball.

- **I was sometimes too slow to tackle issues of underperformance.** It was my least favourite part of the job. (In fairness, I don't know any school leader who enjoys it and, if I did, I certainly would not want to work in their school!) I liked to give people the benefit of the doubt. However, this could lead to a wider perception by staff that 'so and so was getting away with it'.

- **I could be a bit scatty and disorganised.** My desk often resembled a bombsite (unless somebody who was borrowing my office for the day while I was out at a meeting 'helpfully' reorganised my desk to clear some space so that they themselves could work), though I could generally find things.

- **I had comparatively poor IT skills.** To be fair to me, when I came into headship, office PCs were relatively new and laptops a rarity, and those that existed were the size and weight of a slab of granite. The previous generation of heads were simply used to having things typed for them on a typewriter. I did sign up for a skills course at a local college and had to clock in and out. I felt a right muppet, but it really did help me for the advances to come. I really could not manage without Microsoft Word and PowerPoint these days. However, spreadsheets and Excel in particular still represent an absolute nightmare to me. I can just about manage to submit my mileage claims to my accountant quarterly (and that is only because my friend Nick set it up for me), but that is about it!*

If you are ever thinking of booking me to speak, it is worth noting that IT remains my worst nightmare. I was speaking at a conference in Wales for a morning recently. Ten minutes beforehand we could either get a visual feed to the projector or an audio feed to the speakers but not both. Now, I have learned a lot about stress-management through the last ten years but with over 200 people in the room my stress levels were soaring, I can tell you!

My **strengths** included:

- **I had good interpersonal skills** and generally managed to get along with other people well. (Well, possibly with the exception of Joanne, a member of my senior leadership team, who I was convinced was leaking confidential information from meetings to the wider staff in order to undermine my position on topics on which she did not agree with me – or was I a little paranoid at times? OK, add 'could be a little paranoid at times' to the list on the previous page!)

- **I had high levels of empathy for both children and staff.** I really did care greatly. As Dr Andy Cope wrote in the introduction to my book *Ten Traits of Resilience*, I cared too much at times, to my own detriment. I really wanted to create an environment where people would thrive as human beings, not just as labels of 'pupils' and 'staff' – an environment that recognised individual talents and set high expectations but also appreciated that we can all have an off day.

- **I was a creative thinker**, especially when I had other people around me to bounce ideas off. I could come up with some neat solutions to problems when needed. For example, when the local authority was looking to build Phase 8 of my second school (a standalone, four-classroom block and new playground) beyond the main building, nobody seemed to have an issue with the fact that the children would have to cross the drive and staff car park every time they needed to go to the hall in the main building. This would happen at least twice a day for assemblies and lunch, and three times a day on a PE day or if they needed to access one of the IT suites (this was a big school for a primary!). I could see that it would be an accident waiting to happen and suggested that the staff car park be turned into a playground and fenced off from the driveway and that the proposed new playground be changed to a new staff car park. Fairly simple really but nobody else could see it. Well done, James – nobody gets run over and the children have free-flow movement between the two buildings!

- **I was good at strategic thinking.** There were no other primary schools in the county of our size or growing at the rate that we were. It had never been done before and there was no template. I had to anticipate what our needs would be as we grew and then fight tooth and nail to make sure we were given the resources. For example, I convinced the local authority that it was not acceptable for the first aid and medical needs of 800 pupils to be met out of one disabled toilet and chairs in the adjacent corridor. I was also convinced that the modest-sized library that was built when there were around 450 pupils on roll was not fit for purpose, and so the existing library was fitted out as a medical room and a larger library built adjacent to it. Now this was admittedly before the cuts really started to bite so deeply, but nonetheless it took considerable negotiation and persuasion in order to make it happen.

Let's note two things from my revelations above:

1   I have listed six weaknesses and only four strengths and I really had to think about it to come up with four. I feel mildly embarrassed telling you about those. It smacks of blowing one's own trumpet. In common with most school leaders I know, I have a tendency towards high levels of self-criticism and being hard on myself.

2   Strengths that become overexaggerated can soon turn to weaknesses, e.g. I took my empathy to others (a strength) to extremes sometimes, causing me to be slow at times in tackling poor performance (a weakness). Strengths and weaknesses are very much a yin and yang thing.

Personal strengths

There are multiple definitions of the phrase 'personal strengths'. Different people will interpret the term in different ways, which makes it very confusing for the rest of us.

There are ten-plus definitions of the word 'strength' listed in the *Collins English Dictionary*. Among those referring to physical strength, strength of a smell (as in cheese) and the strength of wind (those last two are not connected by the way – just saying) lies this one:

*Someone's **strengths** are the qualities and abilities that they have which are an advantage to them, or which make them successful.*

I think this probably comes closest to what I mean but I am not sure that it covers it all.

For me, I think strengths are the things that you do well and get a kick out of doing.

For example:

1   I could take an assembly and have all the children (and on a good day the staff) absorbed in my story using all my drama training and a variety of props, and varying my delivery, sometimes shouting and at other times whispering so that you could almost hear a pin drop.

2   Governors would sometimes compliment me on the content and style of my headteacher's reports to governors (although probably not always my timing – they were distributed a little close to meetings on occasion!).

3   When I was a deputy head and still had a class of my own, I wrote a pretty good end-of-year report. Parents would often tell me that I had summarised their child really well and got their child off to a tee.

I was good at all three of these things but there was only one of the three that I got a buzz out of doing. Yes, you got it, it was writing my head's report to governors. No, I jest of course; it was actually taking assemblies. It was my 'chocolate time' with the kids amid a day that would involve many meetings, emails and phone calls.

Now, I really don't want to cause any offence to anyone reading this (particularly if you bought this book – I'm less worried if you borrowed it), but when did you ever get to the end of a report to governors and think, 'I had an absolute blast writing that!', or sit at your dining room table on a Sunday in June when all your friends have gone out for the day and think to yourself, 'I am so lucky not to be going out because I am having a ball!'

While I may have been good at numbers 2 and 3, I did them out of necessity and got no real enjoyment from the process. They were things that needed to be done, and with good reason, but they did not get me excited. My assemblies would sometimes overrun and that was because I would lose myself in them and this is what I think happens when you have found a personal strength.

Personal strengths are, I believe, things that we have an aptitude for and where we can pick things up quickly. They energise us and we can easily lose ourselves in them.

Personal strengths can be divided into two groups:

Active strengths: those that we get to use on a regular basis. This is where we get our real enjoyment of the leadership roles.

Passive strengths: these are the things that we are good at and energise us but we seldom get to do. This can be one of the frustrations of leadership. We are promoted because we are good at teaching but the higher up the ladder we go, the less we get to teach.

Tom Rath and Barry Conchie (2008) in their book *Strengths Based Leadership* cite a global Gallup poll that asked the question 'Do you use your strengths every day?' The results may surprise you:

India: 36%
USA: 32%
Canada: 30%
Germany: 26%
UK: 17%

If it's any consolation, the French did even worse, with only 13 per cent.

Weaknesses

And then there are things that we don't perform well in and we find de-energising: my VAT return is one of them. I don't totally understand it and, as Michael, my accountant, will tell you, I often make errors. I am not great with numbers, the time drags when I am doing it and I find it de-energising. That is what characterises a weakness.

Time to reflect

What are the activities that de-energise you even though you are good at them?

-

-

-

What are the activities that de-energise you because you don't perform well in them?

-

-

-

The strengths your staff are looking for

School leaders need a wide variety of strengths in order to do the job effectively. Most staff will forgive you the odd foible, but without a decent range of strengths they are not going to follow you, and without a loyal band of followers you are not going anywhere, except possibly in your dreams. You end up, as the football manager's metaphor goes, 'losing the dressing room'. Now I am no football expert, but we have seen it many times before: successful teams effectively turn on a manager because they have lost faith in their abilities. They don't turn on them aggressively; they simply cease to give of their best. After the miraculous success of Leicester City winning the Premier League, the players seemed to lose faith in Claudio Ranieri the following season and just stopped giving of their best, and we have seen it multiple times with Manchester United in the post-Alex Ferguson era. (Wow, I almost sound like I know what I am talking about, which anyone who knows me will tell you I really do not!)

Truth, compassion, stability and hope

Rath and Conchie (2008) suggest that there are four particular strengths that followers are looking for in their leaders: truth, compassion, stability and hope.

Let's apply this to an education context:

1 **Truth.** Your word is your bond. If you end up conveying the message that your word doesn't mean much, then it will come back to bite you. You only have to look at UK politics to know that this is the case. I am writing this among the Brexit debacle and the May 2019 council elections, where both the two main parties have suffered major casualties as a result of a lack of trust in politicians at a national level. Promises seem to have been broken, whatever your view on the subject may be.

2 **Compassion.** Staff are not looking for the perfect leader. They know that such a thing does not exist, but they are wanting to follow someone at work who genuinely seems to care about them as a person. Staff who feel that way are much more likely to stay, helping to solve the massive retention issue and, by reputation, helping to solve the recruitment issue. Schools gain a reputation not just on their results but, arguably more importantly, on how they treat their staff. People talk. If you don't already, try doing exit interviews with staff who are leaving.

3 **Stability.** OK, I am going to be honest: I didn't always do well on this one. I had a nervous breakdown brought on by work-related stress in 2006–2007 and was off work for six months. (If you want to read more of that story and my subsequent recovery, read my first book *Leading from the Edge*. It's actually a very optimistic read about overcoming difficulties.) Staff are looking for a leader they can count on when times get tough, someone who will act as a buffer to the pointless changes that have categorised education policy in recent years and set clear expectations.

4 **Hope.** This is a basic strength requirement of school leadership but is sometimes overlooked. However good or dire the situation may currently be in school, your staff and your followers need to believe that things can and will get better. It helps them to navigate their way through the chaos of education policy. It's like lighting a beacon to guide travellers through the fog and mist. When leaders appear to be buffeted in every direction by the demands of the job, they convey the impression that they are neither in charge nor in control, but when they initiate action, they signal control and create grounds for optimism.

When hope is absent, people lose confidence, disengage and often feel hopeless.

Rath and Conchie (2008)

Further strengths needed for leadership roles

Having the strengths to meet the needs of your staff is only half the battle of course. Leaders need a raft of other strengths and abilities in order to do the job effectively.

UK-based Mike Roarty and Kathy Toogood (2014) have extensive experience of coaching and working with leadership teams in regional government and with the NHS. They break the strengths needed for leadership roles down into four categories:

1   thinking

2   emotional

3   communication and influencing

4   action and execution.

Within an education context these would include skills such as:

1   Thinking:

- **Analysis** – being able to be objective in a situation, thinking critically and logically.

- **Common sense** – the ability to be pragmatic and down to earth.

- **Creativity** – the ability to find innovative approaches to challenges.

- **Attention to detail** – focusing on the relevant facts and details.

- **Reflection** – the ability to think things through in isolation.

- **Curiosity** – seeking out new ideas and methods in the knowledge that there is always a better way.

- **Strategic thinking** – being able to see the long game, where you want to be and how to get there.

2   Emotional:

- **Emotional intelligence** – the ability to manage your own emotions as well as the ability to read and respond to the emotions of others.

- **Courage** – doing what you know to be right even when it is challenging to do so.

- **Stability** – being able to remain calm when others are losing their heads.

- **Enthusiasm** – a drive and energetic passion that inspires others.

- **Resilience** – the ability to bounce back from adversity and/or the ability to adapt and thrive even when the prevailing winds are not blowing your way.

- **Tenacity** – keeping at a task even when there are significant challenges.
- **Self-confidence** – a belief in your own abilities to lead, tempered with a knowledge that you can always learn and improve (see Chapter 6).
- **Optimism** – a grounded belief that things can and will improve. The ability to see the possibilities in any situation.

3 Communication and influencing:

- **Collaboration** – the ability to share and develop ideas with others towards a common development goal.
- **Communication** – the ability to communicate your ideas to others while actively listening to their opinions and ideas.
- **Persuasiveness** – being able to convince a wide range of stakeholders of the value of an idea or a way of seeing things.
- **Empathy** – being able to read and respond to the emotions of others and respond appropriately to them.
- **Motivator** – energising others to maximise their commitment and contribution towards a given goal.
- **Just** – treating all people fairly and being seen to do so.
- **Inclusive** – including a wide range of staff as appropriate, so that they feel included and engaged.

4 Action and execution:

- **Decisiveness** – being able to take decisions in a timely manner as the situation dictates.
- **Adaptability** – the ability to respond to changing situations and alter plans accordingly.
- **Effectiveness** – getting things done within a strict time frame and with limited resources, while recognising that efficiencies do not always equate with effectiveness (see Chapter 7).
- **Organisation** – being able to work through the practicalities and constraints of school life to ensure that things happen in a timely fashion.
- **Problem-solver** – being 'the barrier removal operative' that solves the problems that stand in the way of your long-term vision.

- **Focused** – keeping your eye on the long-term goals and making sure that short- and medium-term decisions are aligned with them.
- **Self-improvement** – a recognition that you are never the finished article and as such seek new knowledge, skills and ways of thinking to improve the opportunities and outcomes for your pupils.

Time to reflect

Looking at the lists above, consider how you would rate your leadership skills on a scale of 1 to 10 (with 10 being highest) in the following areas:

Skills area	Score
1 Thinking skills	
2 Emotional skills	
3 Communication and influencing skills	
4 Action and execution skills	

Now looking at it in that context, my weaker skills in terms of leadership were:

- **Thinking** – attention to detail.
  I was never a 'doer-finisher'.
- **Emotional** – stability.
  I could sometimes get in a flap under pressure, and though I recovered from my nervous breakdown in 2006–2007, I am sure it did little to enhance my reputation for stability but might have enhanced my reputation for tenacity.
- **Action and execution** – decisiveness.
  I could be quite indecisive at times, particularly if I was tired and feeling fuzzy-minded. As I have said before, almost any decision is better than no decision at all (although as a delegate at a conference reminded me recently, Brexit might well prove to be a notable exception to this rule, whichever side of the debate you might sit on!).

I am very right-brain orientated. The right hemisphere of our brain deals with holistic thought, imagination and creativity, whereas the left hemisphere deals with analysis, logic, science and mathematics.

As a school leader, I knew pretty well what my weaker areas were and set about building a team that would complement my stronger areas and allow me to play to my strengths. Numbers are really not my strong suit. There were no business managers when I first became a head, but as it became more popular, you can bet your bottom dollar I made sure we had one when they did. My senior leadership team consisted of other 'ideas' people, off whom I could bounce ideas, and people who were 'doer-finishers', people who were not necessarily comfortable in front of a crowd but would tear through the work and see things through to a conclusion. Between us we had all four of the strengths above covered.

We had a large governing body in my second headship to reflect the size of the school and were in the fortunate and quite unusual position of not struggling to recruit. Parent governor elections were fiercely contended and, serving a largely middle-class professional community, we had parents with a wide range of skills. We had one who had been an adviser for the local authority some years before and had a good understanding of pedagogy and curriculum issues. Another was a director of a company that specialised in refurbishing pubs and restaurants. He orchestrated the fundraising of the dilapidated training swimming pool and had extensive knowledge of tendering processes, construction and health and safety (no builder ever took us for a ride!). We had a parent governor who was an expert in human resources. You don't need me to tell you that it is a minefield, so this was hugely beneficial. Another was a freelance writer who excelled in drafting letters of persuasion to those who, well, needed persuading. Our vice-chair was a local councillor who usefully had the ear of a number of politicians at county level and our local Member of Parliament. Yet another was a UK director of a major Japanese car manufacturer and what he did not know about financial forecasting and spreadsheets was not worth knowing. It was quite a team and many who had been elected as parent governors stayed on as co-opted or associate governors long after their children had left the school.

I was very lucky because it allowed me, at least some of the time, to play to my strengths.

Leadership is sometimes compared to being like an athlete competing in the decathlon. You have to excel at multiple events in order to win the title but realistically even medal contenders are likely to have one event in which they are less strong.

The training dilemma is: do you put all your efforts into trying to improve your performance in your weaker event, or do you put all your efforts into preparing yourself for the nine events in which you have the most chance of beating the competition? The argument goes that even if you pour all your efforts into your weaker event you may make marginal gains but they would still probably not be enough to win the event; but in so doing you may give your competitors the edge in the other nine as you may be less prepared than you otherwise might be. Result? You lose the overall event.

How does that stack up with you as an analogy? It works for me up to a point. Of course, it is inevitable that we are going to have weaker events, areas in which we are less skilled, but, and it is a big but, we have to *at least* be competent in these areas. I struggled with maths at school and it is still not my forte, so budget-planning always gave me sleepless nights, particularly before we had a school business manager, but I went on courses to make sure I was at the very least competent at it.

I know **Patrick Ottley-O'Connor** has very strong views on this. Speaking exclusively for this book he said, 'It is not good enough to say, for example, "I don't do data". Yes, you need finishers and completers on your leadership team and some who are visionaries who can think outside the box, but don't neglect your own weaknesses; we can and always should be trying to improve ourselves.

Strengths-based leadership

Let's talk more about strengths-based leadership. What do Tom Rath and Barry Conchie (2008) mean by this?

Strengths-based leadership is seen as a method of optimising the efficiency and success of an organisation, in this case a school, by continually focusing on the strengths of people. At its heart is the belief that people have far more potential for growth if they build on their strengths rather than focusing on or fixing their weaknesses. This is not to say that strengths-based organisations ignore people's weaknesses but rather that they focus on developing talents and minimising the effects of weaknesses.

Leaders in strengths-based organisations always invest in their own strengths as well as the strengths of the people they lead. They build well-rounded teams that are collectively strong in all areas and they understand the needs of their followers.

Ekaterina Walter (2013), a writer and expert on strengths-based leadership, suggests that it is human nature to look for the negative. Most of the stories in our daily news bulletins are negative. If you are very lucky you might get a positive, 'feel-good' kind of a story, but largely speaking, it is the negative stories that attract our attention. It is also in our nature to want to fix problems. Many of the great innovations have arisen from a need to solve a problem. Fire, for example, was borne out of a need to keep warm and ward off attackers. The telephone was invented to solve the problem of how to communicate quickly and efficiently over long distances. Even shoe umbrellas (yes, they really do exist but are surely one of the most pointless inventions of all time) were borne out of someone's problem of keeping their expensive shoes dry and clean on a wet day.

The difficulty comes when we take the same approach to evaluating our staff. Walter argues that if we stop trying to 'fix' staff instead of focusing on their strengths and passions we can create an army of followers who passionately believe in a vision and feel empowered to bring it to life.

My friend **Peter Anderton** was Organisational Development Manager for technology giant 3M for nine years. It is a company that encourages staff to use their strengths for ideas and projects that they are passionate about. Years ago, the company introduced '15% time', a programme that encouraged staff to use a portion of their week to develop their own ideas, leading to a number of their bestselling products, including, famously, the Post-it® note. I shudder to think how many of those I get through in a year!

However, the approach is often overlooked, says Ekaterina Walter (2013), because leaders and managers often get stuck in a 'we have always done it this way' style of thinking. She suggests an ABCD approach to leadership.

A: Align rather than fix.

When approaching a new project, look at the skillsets of your staff, have a dialogue with them and try to work out a best fit for a task. Ask for volunteers before you force people to work on something. You may be surprised.

B: Build diverse teams.

Don't be tempted to appoint 'in your own image'. 'Yes people' will not bring the range of diverse ideas needed to be creative and move your school forward.

> *Building a successful team is like building a puzzle. When all the pieces fall into place, you end up with a complete picture.*
>
> Ekaterina Walter (2013)

C: Create a culture of transparency.

When staff trust you, they are likely to be more open about what interests them and what they are passionate about, and if you truly listen to them your followers will give you their best efforts and support.

D: Don't manage, empower.

There is little point in building a diverse team with complementary skills and innovative ideas if you do not empower them to take action. That involves trust, a little risk-taking and a measure of courage. It may also involve some healthy conflict along the way too. The trick and the mark of a good leader is to guide your staff and channel their passions in the right direction without dampening their creativity and enthusiasm.

> *Leadership means encouraging people to live up to their fullest potential and find the path that they love. Only that will create a strong culture and sustainable levels of innovation.*
>
> Ekaterina Walter (2013)

As with any approach to leadership, there are pros and cons of strengths-based leadership.

The pros of strengths-based leadership

- **Creativity.** Knowing and developing the strengths of individuals will give you confidence in delegation, which in turn gives confidence to your team members, encouraging innovation and creativity.

- **It strengthens your position.** As in the decathlon analogy, we all have disciplines in which we are less skilled. Asking for help is not a sign of weakness but a sign of strength. Seeking and accepting the expertise of others builds trust and helps to develop a more consensual approach to leadership, allowing you to focus on what you do best and at the same time promoting effective delegation.

- **It improves staff engagement.** A study by Brian J. Brim and Jim Asplund in 2009 found that organisations that do focus on weaknesses fail to engage a further 22 per cent of their staff (or at least that is the perception of the staff themselves). They have no great weaknesses so the search lights are not shining on them. They feel ignored. These are the people who want to matter but feel like they are just cogs in a machine.

Having that many negative, hostile or miserable employees severely limits what an organisation can achieve.

Brim and Asplund (2009)

Their research goes on to conclude that leaders who focus on the strengths of their staff create a much higher engagement level than those who focus on the negatives. They can achieve a 60:1 ratio of engaged to actively disengaged staff. People want to matter and focusing in on their strengths actually makes them think that they do.

If you were to ask your staff via an anonymous questionnaire whether they would prefer to work in a school focused on their strengths or one that focused on their weaknesses, then I am pretty sure which response you would get. In my view, schools that focus relentlessly on weaknesses, so-called toxic schools, find themselves with staff working to exit at the earliest practicable opportunity. Schools that invest in and develop the strengths of their staff, alongside helping them to improve in the areas in which they are less strong, will have less of a staff retention issue. Nor will they generally have any difficulty recruiting because reputations about the culture of a school spread.

- **Effective recruitment.** A culture that focuses in on strengths will attract applicants because, as I have said, people talk. By losing the 'in my image' approach to the recruitment process, you can focus in on candidates' individual skills instead of finding people who won't rock the boat. This, in turn, allows you to develop a team of people with a diverse range of strengths and attitudes, able, collectively, to tackle anything.

The cons of strengths-based leadership

- **Strengths are a double-edged sword.** As we have already discussed, strengths taken to an extreme can become weaknesses, e.g. delegation can be a strength – empowering staff and making them feel empowered – but, delegation taken to extremes can appear as absolving responsibility, making a leader seem aloof and out of touch.
- **Ignoring weaknesses.** While focusing on strengths can create a diverse and motivated staff, ignoring weaknesses means that staff are unlikely to improve

and this can ultimately undermine the work of the school, particularly when an inspector calls.

- **Achieving consensus.** With everyone playing to their strengths, it can become hard to achieve an overall consensus and, potentially, the larger the staff, the more of an issue this can become.

- **Pigeonholing.** If you concentrate purely on people's strengths, you run the risk of not pushing them outside of their comfort zone. They may not learn new skills and will potentially become bored and frustrated.

The answer, as in many things, lies in moderation. We cannot afford to ignore underperformance, but it needs to be addressed in a constructive and supportive way, and for those clearly no longer up to the changing demands of the job, they need to be allowed to move on with dignity and their contribution to the profession acknowledged. Having said all this, there is compelling evidence that developing the strengths of staff rather than relentlessly focusing on their weaknesses helps to develop a multifaceted staff who want to work for and follow you.

Talking to **Jonny Mitchell**, he emphasised that whether you are a primary head, liaising with two or three other people, or a secondary head, liaising with six or seven other people on a leadership team, it is important to have a spread of strengths, abilities and leadership styles. A successful team firing on all cylinders needs that mix of sometimes differing viewpoints. Jonny says, 'You need someone who is a bit of a Rottweiler, who will sometimes rub people up the wrong way but make people realise that they are not going to get away with poor performance. You need your coaches – people who can signpost and cajole – and you also need to have your judges – those who will come down on one side or the other, those who will give a final decision. With all that, you have a good chance of getting the right sort of outcomes.'

It is May 2019 as I write this. I have just got back from speaking at a conference for 300 school staff at Manchester City's Etihad Stadium. Makes me sound a bit grand and that's really not me, but I was so, so excited! I have spoken at a number of football clubs in the past and even once at Twickenham (a lovely crowd but there were no windows in the room so you couldn't see the pitch – damn, there goes my selfie opportunity). This was something else. A huge, sweeping room overlooking the pristinely mown pitch. The whole stadium was immaculate. This was a premiership club very much at the top of their game.

Speaking before me was Sir John Jones. Knighted in 2003 for his services to education, Sir John worked for most of his professional life in challenging schools across the North West of England, his last post being the headteacher of a large secondary school in Merseyside. I saw him speak some years back as a headteacher and he made me laugh and inspired me in equal measure. He did so again, speaking for an hour and a half without notes (follow on from that, James!).

Being relatively local and a huge Everton fan, he reminded the Manchester audience that it was only a few years ago that City were in the doldrums and that yes, you could get rich investors to plough in large sums of money and build a fantastic stadium, but that in itself would achieve nothing.

It was about people. Having the right leader – in this case, Pep Guardiola, considered to be one of the most successful managers of all time.

Having got the right leader in place, Sir John went on to explain that the recent success of the club was down to four factors:

1 having the right people
2 doing the right things…
3 … in the right way…
4 … for the right reasons.

Listening to Sir John blew me away. As Jim Collins (2001) said about successful organisations in his book *Good to Great*: 'They start by getting the right people on the bus, the wrong people off the bus, and the right people in the right seats… Great vision without great people is irrelevant.'

Summary

- Most school leaders are highly self-critical and often focus on their weaknesses rather than their strengths.
- Strengths are the qualities and abilities you have that give you an advantage.
- Strengths are the things that you do well and you get a buzz out of doing.

Know thyself (part 2)

- The four strengths staff most look for in their leader are: **truth, compassion, stability** and **hope**.
- Successful school leaders need strengths within four categories: **thinking, emotional, communication and influencing,** and **action and execution**.
- As a leader you need to be at least competent in all areas but you don't have to be an expert in everything. Build a team with complementary strengths.
- Optimise the efficiency of your team by focusing on and developing people's strengths.
- Have the right people. Do the right things, in the right way and for the right reasons.
- 'Great vision without great people is irrelevant.'

---

6 Confidence vs humility

Enough confidence to hold your head high, enough humility not to look down on others.

Sonya Teclai

Do you ever, as a leader, have days when you get the distinct impression that you can't do right whatever you do? I know I did.

These days I struggle to remember what I did yesterday, yet alone what happened seven or eight years ago, but among the events I will always remember was one summer's day in my second headship. It was a glorious day and the landscape contractors had mown the school fields in the morning so there was a smell of freshly mown grass everywhere.

I was interviewing all day with governors for a new teacher. There was a bit of a hiatus over lunchtime, which allowed me to catch up with a couple of emails and what had been going on in the rest of the school. Towards the end of lunchtime, a couple of Year 6s reported that they had seen a man parked on the village hall play area adjacent to the school field, taking pictures of children through the mesh fencing. They were reliable kids in my experience and, given that many of our pupils frequented the playground with their parents after school, I thought it prudent to ask the school office to send out a brief letter to parents explaining that, while unconfirmed, I thought that they should know what had transpired.

I went back into the interviews, emerging at around five o'clock unaware that things had really hit the fan. There was near fever-pitch hysteria among parents, the police were involved and had been examining CCTV footage from the village hall and they had identified the number plate of the car and thus the identity of the man. Local BBC Radio were sending a reporter in a mobile broadcasting van with a huge extending aerial on its roof to provide live coverage. The reporter was also a parent at school, and while she was lovely and I always got on well with her, this was doubtless going to be awkward.

Awkward quickly switched to down right uncomfortable when the police turned up before the reporter arrived and revealed that they had interviewed the man taking the photographs.

Awkward No. 1: he was a school parent.

Awkward No. 2: he was not photographing the children at all. He was photographing stone chip damage to the bonnet of his car.

Awkward No. 3: it transpired that the damage to his car had been caused by stones being thrown up over the fence by the tractor mowing the school field!

I cringed. Not my finest hour. The parent concerned was less than impressed at being interviewed by the police, particularly for such a suggested motive. I don't think the family ever forgave me.

When the BBC reporter arrived, she asked me whether I thought I had overreacted. My reply was, 'Well I think you are damned if you do and damned if you don't!'

If I had not warned parents about a possible safeguarding threat on a public playground and something had actually happened, I would never have forgiven myself (and nor, incidentally, would they!) but as it worked out, I was open to accusations of hysteria, whipping up a minor media storm and striking the fear of God into a lot of parents. I was never going to win on that one, and although for the most part I loved my 23 years in school, it was not always easy to get things right.

This was very much true of striking the balance between confidence and humility. Staff want polar opposites from us at the same time. They want us to be able to project confidence and be clear about our vision and direction of travel, as well as making our expectations clear, so that there can be no misunderstandings. Our confidence gives them confidence and yet, if we take our self-confidence too far, we run the risk of coming over as being overconfident, or possibly even arrogant. So, staff need us to project humility, but coming over as being too humble we run the risk of people believing that we lack confidence. It's a tricky one!

I would certainly not like to be perceived as arrogant, but I am sure that some people along my career journey (beginning to sound like *X Factor* here!) would have seen me as such. I was seconded by our local authority to be acting deputy head of a large primary school after only three years of teaching. I was encouraged after a term to apply for the substantive position and got it. I was very young and very inexperienced in teaching in general, yet alone in leadership. While appreciating the faith placed in me by the head, whom I greatly admired, deep down I knew I was woefully under-skilled and was very conscious that a good number of the teaching staff were twice my age. So, I projected a confidence that was not truly there deep down and made some decisions that did little to endear me to them, for example allocating stationery resources by department rather than in a central store cupboard – it became known as 'Papergate'! I didn't listen to other leaders who had been there far longer and probably came over as an arrogant upstart.

I have mellowed over the years and progressed beyond managing the paper cupboard! Lessons learned. I was actually trying to mask my lack of confidence by projecting the extreme opposite. I suspect that we all do that from time to time.

Confidence

There is no doubt in my mind that you have to have a certain level of self-confidence in order to even apply for a leadership role, let alone carry it out. You have to have a certain level of self-belief, and yes, that may get buffeted from time to time by the ups and downs that inevitably form part of school life. Yes, that confidence will ebb and flow at times, just as waves lap upon the seashore, and yes, sometimes we have to be consummate actors as leaders, projecting a level of confidence to staff that we may not be feeling deep down at that moment. Our confidence gives them confidence and, if the waters are a little bit choppy, they will need someone to reassure them and upon whom they can depend. Our self-confidence may sometimes feel a little buried under the sand but, fundamentally, it does need to be there.

You see, school leaders are, in my experience, appointed more so for their confidence than their humility. Rightly or wrongly, I believe that to be the case. Recruitment panels are looking for people with a clear and appealing vision and who create the impression that they have enough faith in their own skills and strengths to make that vision more than a document or a PowerPoint presentation, but to actually make it come alive. The very same confidence that has allowed you to be effective as a member of a teaching team is what allows you to step forward, step up to the plate and lead other staff.

However, there is a harsh reality: staff want to follow confident leaders; I have yet to meet anyone who really wants to follow an arrogant one.

Anyone who knows me well will tell you two interconnected things about me:

1. I have a very poor sense of spatial awareness. For example, some years back I bought two new desks from IKEA to re-equip the main school office. One was a left-hand wave desk and the other a right-hand one. Richard, my deputy at the time, worked on the right-hand wave desk, while I worked on the left-hand wave. The difficulty was that the instructions (which I usually ignore, except in case of emergencies) were written as generic for both orientations but were actually written as if you were constructing the right-hand wave version. I really could not transpose diagrams through 180° in my mind and eventually had to resort to finding a mirror to reflect the instructions into what I actually saw in front of me.

2. I have absolutely no sense of direction. Truly. I get lost in Premier Inns, which I spend a lot of time in when I'm away speaking at conferences and INSETs. I love the fact that they are good value, you know exactly what you are going to get, and the staff are friendly and helpful. But all the corridors look the same! I get lost! I can't read a map well either. In the days before sat navs, I was seconded by the local authority to visit and support NQTs, many of whom were in very small primary schools in villages I had never heard of in the depths of the Peak District. I had to work out two versions of my mileage claim: the miles I had *actually* done and the miles the local authority would *believe* to be credible. (I got so, so lost.)

The fact is that these days I rely on my sat nav to get me where I need to be. Except…

I currently drive a Renault Megane Sports Tourer (posh title but basically an estate to accommodate my huge golden retriever, Eddie, around whom much of my world revolves). I love the car and test drove one before placing an order. However, the one thing you don't tend to try out on a test drive is the sat nav. It is rubbish! It often does not anticipate traffic jams. It cannot cope with the unexpected, such as a Premier Inn on an industrial or commercial park with no recognisable postcode. It leads me down one-track lanes with no hope of a passing space and even through fords. It does not provide me with a clear sense that it knows what it is doing. It is not helped that it is voiced by someone who sounds like Theresa May. My sat nav sounds like a startled rabbit, unsure of which way to turn and often advocating a U-turn at the next available opportunity. It does not fill me with confidence.

So, these days I use the Google Maps app on my phone as my sat nav. It can find the most obscure hotels and locations, it anticipates the traffic jams and provides me with alternative routes well in advance of any problems, and works out the better roads to take me on, avoiding single-track roads with no passing spaces *and* fords (the water crossings, not the cars!). The voice exudes clarity and confidence and although she makes the odd mistake, I can forgive her. She has my confidence and so I know I can trust her, and I will happily follow her directions.

Why is self-confidence so important?

People will simply not follow a leader who has no confidence in themselves. Self-confidence is central to school leadership. Without it you are essentially building a house without any foundations. Sure, you can make it look very grand with balconies, sliding glass doors and a beautifully painted façade, but without the foundations of self-confidence the building will come tumbling down sooner or later (probably sooner!).

As **Patrick Ottley-O'Connor** once reminded me, as a leader you are paid to make decisions. You may listen to the advice of others and draw upon your team's strengths but ultimately the decisions are yours. You have to be confident in yourself and your abilities in order to make those decisions, otherwise you will procrastinate and be afraid to commit. You can build a great team, be a good communicator and empower others, but without self-confidence it is all likely to be to no avail.

When I was unwell over ten years ago and suffering from chronic stress and anxiety, I was not a very effective leader for a time. I slept badly and that affected my decision-making, agonising over decisions (a common response to stress) and often going for the safe option instead of taking calculated risks in order to do what was right. This was the very antithesis of being a bold leader and it was certainly not the usual me. Leaving a salaried position as a head to set up as a speaker and author took some courage and faith that the work would come in (which thankfully it continues to do – phew!) but it is a natural instinct to stay with what is familiar, which is why some teachers cling on even though they have lost the passion and fire in their belly that they once had. For them the yacht of education has set sail for new ports, leaving them standing on the harbour wall. These are the people who need to be encouraged to leave, but leave with dignity.

So, why else is self-confidence so important in school leadership?

- Self-confidence not only allows you to make the tough calls in a considered but timely fashion but it also inspires confidence in other staff. It enables you to lead a staff meeting or deal with parental complaints with authority.

- It also allows you to accept feedback and, as **Hannah Wilson** said, have those fierce conversations without feeling threatened and being defensive.

- It enables you to deliver a passionate and inspiring eve-of-inspection speech to staff that will rally the troops behind you rather than seeing through empty words that display a lack of certainty.

- Confidence gives leaders the courage to do what is right rather than what is easy, taking decisions that align with the long-term vision for where the department or school needs to get to.

- It allows them to communicate effectively, choosing their words carefully to motivate and empower their followers.
- Confidence allows leaders to trust in their own capabilities and believe in their own ability to eventually resolve even the most challenging of situations.
- It allows them to see setbacks as temporary rather than regarding them with permanence.
- Confident leaders will remain calm in even the most challenging situations, and while they may well experience fear, they will do what is right anyway.
- Confident leaders will make mistakes, as everybody does, but they will hold their hands up to them with staff and learn from them.
- Self-confident school leaders take a little more than their fair share of the blame and a little less than their fair share of the credit.
- Confident leaders will make members of the team feel valued and important, with a clear role to play.
- Confident school leaders have a grounded ambition for what their staff and pupils can achieve together.

As **Angela Browne** said, talking exclusively for this book, 'Self-confidence doesn't mean you get things right all the time, nor that you have all the answers. It's about saying to yourself, "I don't *know* that I can but I will give it my all. I will put myself at the front of the school and give it my best shot at taking it in the right direction." However, there must be self-reflection. People will not have confidence in your confidence if there is no self-reflection or admission of mistakes.'

So, confidence is the foundation of successful school leadership and that is all well and good. I have yet to meet anyone who would not like to be confident, leader or not, and yet the reality is that sometimes our confidence deserts us. I was terribly anxious when both of my previous books were published. I was very quiet in the days leading up to publication, worried about how the books would be received and what the reviews might say. Fortunately, they were received very well but I know I will be exactly the same when this book sees the light of day rather than being confined to my rather (OK, very) untidy office. We will always have moments of self-doubt and anyone who doesn't I suspect is either a) not telling the truth or b) delusional.

When was the last time you seriously doubted yourself professionally or personally?

What were the circumstances?

How did it make you feel in yourself?

What did you do to challenge and overcome that self-doubt?

14 ways to boost your self-confidence as a leader

So, let's consider some ways to boost your confidence when you are experiencing moments of doubt.

1. Remember, people appointed you because they had faith in you

You are not where you are by accident. Remind yourself that you were appointed to this position because other people, i.e. the selection panel, believed in you and your ability to deliver on the demands of the job. Prove them right. Don't second-guess yourself.

2. List your accomplishments

Most of us are not very good at boasting so we often brush our achievements under the carpet because we don't want to appear arrogant. The one time we do it is when we apply for a new position. We dust off our application letter and update our achievements, making it applicable to the role we are applying for in the hope of impressing the selection panel. Don't wait until the next time you apply for a job; update that list regularly.

Time to reflect

List five things, however small, that you have achieved professionally in the last 12 months.

1.

2.

3.

4.

5.

Just the act of reminding yourself of what you have achieved and the difficulties you have overcome is an instant boost to your self-confidence.

3. Step outside your comfort zone

As I have said before, if you don't step outside your comfort zone it shrinks when you want it to grow. I try to push myself professionally to do things I have not done before.

I spoke recently at a conference in South Wales. 300 heads had signed up for the event, more than the organisers had achieved the previous two years. I was a little worried if I am being honest. I have spoken at a lot of conferences in Wales in recent years and pointed out to the organisers (who were lovely!) that some of the participants may well have heard me before. They smiled at me and said that they were well aware that some would have heard me before, because they had told them so! They said that they were coming because they wanted to hear me again. It brought a lump to my throat to be honest. My presentations have evolved over time like a comedian develops a set on tour; you try out new material and see what works. If you get a good response you keep it in; if you don't you drop it. The challenge was to keep the same core messages around wellbeing that people had enjoyed the first time around, while having enough new material that people were not sitting there thinking, 'I have heard all this before!' The event did take me outside my comfort zone but it was very well received and I felt stronger and more confident for having done it.

Even after years of public speaking I still get really nervous beforehand and sometimes even nauseous. I don't think that will ever go away. (Actually, I don't want it to; the one time I did not experience any nerves was the one time it went really badly.) I just accept that the nerves are part of the process and that in a couple of hours' time and with some positive feedback from the audience (I don't tend to get a ten-minute standing ovation or have roses thrown on stage, admittedly, but people do really seem to connect with what I am trying to say), I will be buzzing.

The point is this: the more used you are to stepping outside your comfort zone, the more comfortable you will become with, well, being uncomfortable.

4. Be clear about your strengths and areas for development

Knowing what you are good at and what areas you need to ask for help with will bring both clarity and confidence. (See Chapter 6 of *Ten Traits of Resilience* for more on asking for help.)

5. Link up with someone else who is a leader but outside of your immediate situation

That may be somebody in a different department or even a different school. When your ideas are at a formative stage, you may not be ready to spill them in front of others just yet. Using someone else as a sounding board helps you to check through your thinking and get an outside perspective. You can ditch impracticable ideas and refine those that are a goer. This improved clarity of thoughts and ideas will also build confidence.

6. Build a network of contacts

It is important to raise your head above your own particular furrow and see what other people are up to in different contexts. To do this face to face is great if you can, but social media, while often maligned, can be a great source of support, joining up people with a huge range of ideas and experience not only in the UK but from around the world. A number of people I have met in the course of my writing, including **Rae Snape**, **Ritesh Patel and Lisa Lea-Weston**, are people that I initially met on Twitter. They have been an invaluable source of ideas, encouragement and support.

A cautionary note though. Support is a two-way street. It is easy, when times are good, to overlook our network of contacts. We feel more relaxed and complacent and less likely to engage with our support network. And then things hit the fan and we need support, perhaps from a more experienced colleague. You have to invest in these relationships. A strong network can be a huge source of support when you need it and it will boost your confidence when times are not so good because you will know you are not alone. Remember that isolation is the biggest enemy of resilience.

7. Be self-aware

Build in time in a week to take stock. Make sure you are clear on your leadership strengths. Seek out feedback from people, and not just from 'Yes' people (as my friend **Peter Anderton** would say, you need to avoid appointing in your own image and ending up with a staff of 'mini-mes' who see the world exactly like you do). Honest feedback will help you to clarify your areas of strength and where you need to improve. The added bonus is that leaders who seek feedback will appear more confident than those who avoid it. This in turn inspires confidence in you from your team.

8. Plug your gaps

High pressure combined with low skill levels leads to stress. Yes, you should own your strengths but own your weaknesses too. Address them. Find some professional development that will help you improve. Yes, budgets are squeezed so tightly at present, but it does not have to be an expensive course necessarily. Spending time working alongside or shadowing a colleague skilled in one of your weaker areas, be they in your school or in another, will increase your knowledge and skills base, helping you to feel more confident. Finance was my Achilles' heel when I started out as a head but, by working on improving my knowledge and understanding, I became competent and, without tooting my own trumpet too much, I was pretty good at it and could hold my own in complex budget meetings with the local authority.

9. Keep track of your priorities for the week

I have rarely met a school leader who was not really busy, and if they were not, they were probably not doing the job well. Most leaders have a 'to-do' list as long as their arm (well two arms actually). The temptation (and I know because I did it at times) is to complete lots of quick actions so that you can tick more off the list, but in doing so you are often completing low-impact actions first. Ask yourself whether this is the best use of your time. Are there some items on the list that would have a bigger impact but they are the can that 'keeps getting kicked down the street'?

10. Ask for help where it is needed

Knowing where and when you need input from others is important. Yes, you are paid to make the final decisions (and of course how swiftly a decision needs to be made), but gathering more information and the views of trusted colleagues will help you to make decisions with greater conviction. (For more on this see *Ten Traits of Resilience*, Chapter 5, 'Decisiveness' and Chapter 6, 'Asking for help'.)

11. Build your team up

Schools are often very good at celebrating the achievements of their pupils but less so the successes of their staff. Try a celebration pre-school staff briefing on a Friday morning. It will be a feel-good ten to 15 minutes that lets everyone celebrate everything good that has happened that week and allows people to go into the weekend on a positive note. It helps to build a school-wide culture of celebrating effort and achievement. Moreover, it will build the confidence of your team and your confidence in them. The greater the confidence you have in the team around you and in their support for you, the higher your levels of self-confidence are likely to be.

12. Break things down into smaller goals

Try not to get overwhelmed by big projects.

I can remember as a child in the early 1970s that my dad, who was managing director of a family business of shoe shops called, appropriately enough, Hilton's Shoes, took up golf. He had no real experience, but a lot of business seemed to be done on the golf course in those days (probably still is for all I know – I don't move in those kinds of circles). My dad enlisted my help one Saturday as his caddy. I had recently been dropped from the school football club. (No, not the school football *team*, the actual *club*. Apparently, I showed little promise in turns, falling over and 'playing the man not the ball' and rarely actually connecting with the ball!) So, I had a sudden window in my diary on Saturday mornings. Now I loved my dad to bits but his golfing skills gave my footballing ones a run for their money and he was approaching his first 18-hole match against other players (well, I suppose that's what made it a match). As his willing but struggling caddy, I had trudged behind him to the first tee. There were no golf buggies back then and even if there had been, I would not have been of an age to drive one. He had inherited my grandfather's clubs, made in the 1930s, which were seemingly forged out of lead and kept in a bag without even wheels. Bear in mind I was only a couple of years older than the photograph you saw of me at the front of the book. I was struggling a little here but my dad, although he was the best dad in the world, was largely oblivious. He was focused on trying to get around the 18-hole course. I sensed he was apprehensive (although I probably did not know the word at the time, let alone know how to spell it!) but as he was about to tee off, he said out loud, 'One hole at a time.'

Whether my dad was talking out loud to himself or talking to me, it stuck with me. Rather than being overwhelmed by the pressure and the watching gaze of the other players, he broke the task down into 18 smaller goals. I don't remember him winning but he did get around the course.

Enough said.

13. Aim for respect and not popularity

Nobody I know deliberately seeks to be unpopular but doing the right thing will not be popular, as other members of staff are only likely to have some of the pieces of the jigsaw and our nature is to look to see how things are going to affect us first. Accepting that this is the way of things can help to build your confidence. You have the bigger picture, for example balancing the ideal with financial constraints. Trust your instincts.

14. Be kind to yourself

Nobody knows everything. No leader has a crystal ball. To a certain extent we are all bluffing it but seek to minimise the risks by building a strong team, addressing our weaknesses and growing in knowledge and as a leader.

So, I hope I have successfully made the case for the need for school leaders to have a good level of self-confidence, as well as suggesting some ways of building yours further. However, any strength taken to the extreme is likely to end up being a weakness. Overconfident leaders run the risk of being perceived as being arrogant.

Arrogance

Arrogant school leaders (and I have met one or two over the years but, for obvious reasons, I am not going to name them here) often think (or at least are perceived as thinking) that they have all the answers. If you have all the answers, you don't need to listen to the ideas of other people. So, for a while they will continue to offer them, but they reduce to a trickle. Then they stop because your staff realise it is a pointless waste of energy. It is futile. You either don't listen or you listen until there is a pause, where you can jump in and re-state your position and ultimately go ahead and do whatever it was you were going to do anyway!

There are a number of problems with this style of leadership:

- Arrogant leaders are difficult to trust. On the rare occasions they appear to be listening to you, you will always doubt their sincerity. It is difficult to respect someone you do not trust, and without either trust or respect you are on a very slippery slope and people will be happy to sell you down the river.
- With an ideas pool limited to a circle of one, you are limited to recycling your own thinking and closing the door to a range of opinions and ideas that might just enhance your own, or be different and actually be better.
- You may miss flaws in your own plans, the danger signs that actually something might go badly wrong if you are not willing to listen. Imagine you were going backpacking in the Peak District and someone in your group

spotted that you were the only person without a sleeping bag strapped to their rucksack; you would want them to tell you, wouldn't you? Well, if they don't trust or respect you and you don't listen anyway, they aren't going to say anything, and it can be awfully cold in the Peaks at night!

Humility

So, let's turn our attention to the subject of humility. I think humility sometimes gets a bit of a bad press, as being of questionable value in leadership terms. We have already established that you need a level of confidence to lead or even manage people, and that staff are looking for confidence in a leader to give them confidence themselves in the direction of travel and the value of their contribution to that journey.

Confidence and humility are not polar opposites. As with many things it comes down to clarity of terminology, so I want to dispel some myths and talk first about what I think humility *isn't*.

Humility does not mean that you lack confidence, nor that you have low self-esteem or are meek and timid. It does not mean that you are submissive or unassertive. Nor is it constantly putting yourself down in front of other people. If it were these things it would present something of a conundrum, as how could you be all these things and yet be a confident leader? And we know that confidence is valued as a virtue. But that is not what humility in leadership is all about.

Humility does not mean you think less of yourself. It means you think of yourself less.
Unknown (credited to many)

I love this quote, sometimes attributed to C. S. Lewis, but whoever wrote it, they are wise words and come the closest to summing up what humble leadership means to me.

I was interviewing **Rae Snape**, Headteacher at the Spinney Primary School in Cambridge, about this whole confidence and humility in leadership thing and she said this to me: 'I describe myself as Head Learner. I am brain motivated to find out more. I am constantly assessing and... I am confident, I don't know everything! To quote Pierre Levy, "No one knows everything, everyone knows something, and that's why we need to learn." I carry a bag of Lego® around with me. Why? Because it is a wonderful metaphor for building relationships and connecting with people. I have the **humility** to know that I do not know everything and the **confidence** to know that I can still learn.' Wise words indeed!

Humility is also about actively listening to people. As NAHT past president Kim Johnson once reminded me, we have two ears and one mouth for a reason. This actually marks the difference between the confident but humble leader and the arrogant one. The former actively and consistently listens to the views of others and gives due credit to the ideas and successes of the team. Arrogant leaders may try to give the impression that they are listening but rarely take on board what is said, nor are they comfortable with the concept of deflected glory, preferring to be in the limelight themselves.

I know, I am not the first – and I certainly will not be the last – educationalist to draw upon the work of Jim Collins for inspiration. He is perhaps best known as the author of *Good to Great: Why Some Companies Make the Leap… and Others Don't.* Following five years of research, and backed up with hard evidence, Collins (2001) explores the many variables that act as enablers to organisations moving from being 'good' to, well, 'great'. While it is true that much of the book explores the world of commerce, many of the underlying principles are equally applicable to the world of education.

Collins suggests that there are five levels of leadership, culminating in 'Level 4: Effective Leader' and 'Level 5: Executive'. The term 'executive head' has become increasingly common in recent years. Ten years ago, nobody would have known what on earth you were talking about and even now it means different things in different contexts, so let's not get drawn into a debate on the meaning of job titles or we will be here all night. At Level 5, Collins is talking about *great* leaders and what sets them apart from *effective* leaders.

> A Level 5 leader – an individual who blends extreme personal humility with intense professional will.
>
> Jim Collins (2001)

In other words, Level 5 leadership is humility plus drive.

What Collins found in his research was that the Level 5 leaders were not people with massive egos who wanted to be placed upon a pedestal or become larger-than-life iconic heroes.

> They were seemingly ordinary people quietly producing extra-ordinary results.
>
> Jim Collins (2001)

Level 5 leadership is not just about modesty and humility, he argues; it is also about an unwavering drive to do whatever is needed to make their organisation great.

Great school leaders are ambitious for their schools and not for themselves.

Robert I. Sutton (2010), in his book *Good Boss, Bad Boss*, builds on Collins' ideas. He suggests that *great* leaders will be driven to achieve two types of goals:

- Firstly, **performance**.

They do everything within their power to help their team do great work and achieve great results (think back to the analogy of school leaders as 'barrier removal operatives' on page 50).

- Secondly, **humanity**.

They do everything they can to make sure that their team regularly experiences pride and always experiences dignity (especially if there is to be a parting of the ways and someone needs to move on).

> *Working with dignity... [is] taking actions that are worthy of respect by oneself and others.*
>
> Randy Hodson (2001)

Sutton goes on to point out that the judgement of the success of the leader in achieving these two goals is not best carried out by the leader themselves (although I do believe that self-reflection and self-evaluation are vital in school leadership!). He suggests that the final evaluation on the *performance* of an organisation should not come from an insider but that the evaluation of the *humanity* of the leader should probably come from within. Why? Because many people in life generally suffer from what is termed 'self-enhancement bias'. In Sutton's studies, he found that 90 per cent of all drivers believe they possess above-average driving skills and, surveying senior leaders in schools in the USA, 70 per cent believed they possessed above-average leadership skills! (Interestingly, only two per cent reported having below-average leadership skills. I wonder why?!)

As with all things, it is a matter of balance. In conversation for this book, **Jonny Mitchell** said of confidence and humility, 'Sometimes you have to put yourself up there as confident whether you are feeling it or not. As heads we want to be thought of as being humble. Hero headteachers might work in some situations but it's about cooperating and giving credit where credit is due. We want people to be treated equally and democratically. You have got to have some humility in there.'

- What are your thoughts on confidence and humility in school leadership?

- How do you balance the two?

It is important to display confidence, but a level of humility is what allows you to connect with your staff and accept that we are all in this together. Get the balance wrong and it can have dire consequences *but* get it right and the possibilities for success are endless. Therein lies the challenge of great school leadership.

Summary

- School leaders are often damned if they do and damned if they don't. You have to learn to live with it. It goes with the territory.
- Staff want balance from their leaders. They expect you to project confidence but be humble at the same time.
- Any virtue (including confidence and humility), taken to extreme, becomes a weakness.
- While your confidence will ebb and flow, you do need a level of self-belief to operate effectively.
- Arrogant leaders find it difficult to gain trust and it is very difficult for a school to move forward in the absence of trust.
- Humility does not mean that you lack confidence or have low self-esteem.
- Effective school leaders balance personal humility with high levels of professional willpower.
- Great school leaders are ambitious for their schools rather than for themselves.

Confidence vs humility

7 Efficiency vs effectiveness

We live in deeds, not years; in thoughts not breaths; in feelings, not in figures on a dial. We should count time by heart throbs…

Aristotle

Do you remember when you started? Day one, ground zero? Your first day as a teacher, as a head, as a new member of staff? I do – the mixture of excitement and fear. Terrifying but exhilarating.

> I will never forget my first day as a headteacher. It was all about people: greeting the staff, the parents at the gate, the pupils! Many of them I already knew, having been deputy at the school for eight years.
>
> I recall those first interactions as we sized each other up, trying to find the strands of conversation to connect on common ground. People were analysing me, trying to read me – to see whether much had changed in the intervening six weeks between being deputy and head. As the first days and weeks passed and we began to settle into our new relationships, there was an increased momentum, as we evolved together, beginning to write new chapters.

> I have always thought that those first, formal and informal one-to-ones with colleagues were so useful – filled with honesty and opportunity. Staff were unconcerned about sharing their thoughts on the past – good and bad – and what the future might hold, because they knew and trusted me. No awkward first dances then, but good, constructive conversation and optimism.

For new leaders, the relationships evolve; there is the sharing of new ideas and a sense of action and purpose. This becomes a job you love, are energised by; for all the bad news stories and scepticism, this school, this job, your tenure is different. Good people, great community... hope! You feel of value, effective. But...

As you see out your second year of nativities, sports days and parents' evenings, things often don't feel quite the same. You wake at 6 am to the sounds of birdsong or Erik Satie or whatever else 'Alexa' has chosen for you. You haven't really slept; after waking at 2 am to nip to the loo, the chink of light at the back of your consciousness became a full-on neon headlight and off went budget, head's report and, yes, your favourite member of staff, Mrs bloody Jones, all pinging around in your head!

At 7 am your phone buzzes as you brush your teeth; a text from Mrs (b.) Jones announces that she is going to be off again. What's the reason this time? Because her goldfish appears listless and she is beside herself? You can't afford cover, so you set to work rinsing your mouth and working out whether you have a spare teaching assistant or someone you could persuade to give up their PPA, or whether you could split the class or set aside your day and teach them yourself.

By 8 am you're in, the site supervisor is scrubbing the last of the spray-paint graffiti from the brick wall next to the fading mural of children playing on a summer's day and you are in your office, looking for your thermal mug, which you are sure you put in the drying rack in the staffroom the night before. It's the third one that has mysteriously disappeared this year! Then it's off to the 'C' block toilets to try to figure out why the urinals are stuck on permanent flush.

By 10 am, following a run-in with a parent who wants you to know how much you and your staff have destroyed his daughter's life because she didn't get a solo in the upcoming Comic Relief concert, you can finally settle down to... data.

Despite everything and your best intentions, your relentless efforts to be efficient, to ensure that your school runs like clockwork, you find yourself floundering, having fallen overboard, swept under by the currents of the uncontrollable.

Now don't get me wrong; this is, hopefully, not an illustration of a normal day, but it can easily begin to feel like it and many of you, I suspect, will relate to the scenario that I set out above. Life has become that battle between reactive and proactive leadership that I referred to in my last book, *Ten Traits of Resilience*. It can be so sapping on your time, your love of the job and your very wellbeing. It is why a focus on, commitment to and mastery of the balance between efficiency and effectiveness is so crucial as a school leader, not only professionally, but personally too. How you balance the two can define the success or otherwise of what you and your community work so hard to try to achieve.

The ability to execute and get things done as a leader can be a key driver to success, but can also, ultimately, lead to your downfall. It can result in unintended and unforeseen costs for the school, your colleagues and you.

Efficiency is important and can, of course, result in high levels of sustained productivity. However, the high levels of efficiency that enable highly task-focused leaders to be so productive often come at a price and, more often than not, at the expense of relationships, the shared ownership of vision, values and purpose, and the interactions that inspire a team, allowing them to feel valued, supported and developed. The empathy necessary in great leadership can fall by the wayside.

Patrick Ottley-O'Connor is currently the Interim Executive Head at North Liverpool Academy. He is an expert in supporting schools in trouble and talks of the importance of balance, saying, 'They are complementary. If you are efficient, you can be more effective and vice versa.' **Angela Browne**, Interim Deputy CEO at Castle Hill Academy Trust, who so poignantly appeared in the BBC documentary series *School*, warned that 'People fall by the wayside sometimes, because we don't have time to nurture staff into effectiveness.' She goes on to reflect that 'We all want to feel valued and effective and on the journey to being better at things. We have to hope to build systems that build effectiveness that then leads to efficiencies.'

Leaders who focus too much on efficiency in order to 'get things done', a leadership style referenced in Daniel Goleman's (2017) iconic book *Leadership That Gets Results*, are leaders who end up being less effective overall. The pace of change and uncertainty sees to that.

The idea of creating and implementing one system and then focusing relentlessly on its delivery can work in automated and traditionally industrial environments; but in schools, where so much is about the organic and unpredictable nature of people, and with so many variables (for instance, budget and policy are often beyond your control and at the mercy of the increasingly bizarre four-to-five-year political cycles), the relentless pursuit of the one working model often leads to burnout.

Kronos (2017), one of the world's leading HR management companies, produced a report into 'The employee burnout crisis'. It highlighted that 95 per cent of HR leaders cited burnout (driven by a relentless focus on efficiency) as being the biggest threat to employee engagement and ultimately high staff turnover.

Sustainable leadership is about being able to balance getting things done along with inspiring and empowering people – the balance between leading efficiently but also effectively. If you are too efficiency focused, you develop tunnel vision around the achievement of tasks and results to the detriment of what makes leadership successful, purposeful and sustainable. You need to have the ability to see things strategically through a broader lens, which can inform a change of pace or direction, to have the ability to implement and amend your vision in practice. It is leaders who achieve this balance – task- and people-focused – who realise that schools can only succeed by being both efficient and effective.

The difficulty is that outside drivers, such as budget reductions in real terms, often push us to become efficiency-driven. A recurring issue with efficiency-focused leaders (and believe me, I learned this the hard way) is that they tend to feel largely reactive and therefore under constant pressure, and as a result, they can become controlling, have difficulty devolving responsibility and therefore disenfranchise staff, which leads to alienation, isolation and even sometimes a little paranoia. There have been times when I have succumbed to this style of behaviour and walked around my school, into the staffroom and to the gate believing that people were talking about me and my actions. (They probably were!)

Time to reflect

Has there ever been a point in your career when your actions have left staff feeling disenfranchised?

What actions caused those feelings?

What were the main drivers behind your actions?

Looking back, what would you do differently?

It is such an easy trap to fall into; we are raised to believe that to demonstrate our value and worth we must work hard, stay late and give up weekends. When I was a student, I would often hear other people talking about how much revision they were doing heading towards exams, and I was intimidated by some who claimed to be working 30-hour days... there aren't even 30 hours in a day! In a way, it is a flaw of the traditional education system. We are raised to see so much of what we do and learn as a solo pursuit, which can lead to a fear in later life that inhibits our ability to trust others. If I don't do it myself, it won't be done right; I will undermine my own value.

In those early days of school leadership, most of us have no choice but to rely upon and trust our colleagues; they know the school and the community better than we do, and others on the leadership team may have been in post longer than you and have had time to understand the cultural foibles and challenges of your community (and there are always some!). I remember once being told by a very experienced head that I would only really feel 'in control' when I had been through a whole cycle of the school year in post. She was right and that is often the danger point. As a new leader, it is expected that you will need support, seek advice and make mistakes, but the more a part of the furniture you become, the more you perceive that the expectations of you change. The honest conversations of those early halcyon days have become more guarded. You feel a greater expectation to 'know' and to 'have the answer'. You can end up in a position where people have become so dependent on you because you have felt the need to control so much, and so often for the right reasons. In order to take pressure off them, you have created a culture where people go through you for everything, even gifting you their problems, in the belief that you are the only person who can solve them.

Some leaders believe that their role is to make themselves indispensable to the school; they feel a deep responsibility that comes from their pay grade. We have all been there. If we find ourselves on a rare professional development day, we call school during the lunchbreak to make sure that we aren't needed. What effective leaders realise, though, is that leadership is about endeavouring to do yourself out of a job by transferring responsibility, and most importantly trust, so that you can be at your most efficient: driving evolution and ensuring the delivery of vision, values and collegiate purpose. When people talk about sustainable and effective leadership, it is surely this.

It is, of course, far easier said than done, especially in the current climate – one where schools have never been under greater scrutiny and greater strain. These are very stormy seas indeed. Like a troubled business, many are forced to focus on trying to balance budgets, improve data and make decisions while simply trying to survive. There are times when you as a leader must make the strategic call to focus on efficiency, and that is right, but the key is to be able to audit your behaviour and process so that you don't end up trapped in a loop that will lead to burnout.

Time to reflect

In the last working week, how often do you think you have been reactive?

As a result, what short-, medium- and long-term actions could you consider in order to make more of your time and allow you to become more proactive?

Ask others to help

Find five colleagues you trust and have good relationships with, from across the school, not just from your leadership team.

- Ask them how well they think you balance reactive focus versus proactive focus.

- Ask them to quantify it by a notional percentage and to give you examples of when you are at your best and at your worst.

You are not alone

Remember, because you work in a school, you are surrounded by experts in coaching and human leadership; they will know how to help. In the corporate world, CEOs pay huge amounts of money for what your staff can help you with.

Relationships and the development of trust are vital to your ability to lead with balance; therefore taking time to nurture that climate is vital, not just at the start of your tenure but throughout your career. Difficult, I know, but try to build time into your week for professional reflections with others, where there can be no distractions, so maybe off site if that is feasible. This may not come naturally, or even feel comfortable at first, but having opportunities to reflect and self-reflect is so valuable. It is far too easy to develop the tunnel vision that leads to obsessions with efficiency.

Mindfulness has become somewhat of a buzzword, but it is such an important quality in a successful leader: that ability to self-reflect, in real time. To be able to audit whether you are doing the right thing for the right reasons, whether you are making decisions based on avoiding the real issue or acting too quickly in order to appear efficient and decisive.

One of the most common things I hear from colleagues is that they have a certain character type that drives their leadership and therefore defines their approach. People might say that they are good at efficiency, or that they are bad at delegating. The good news is that these colleagues have accomplished some level of self-awareness but they need to take the next step and do something about it! The problem with labels is that they can lead you to limit your beliefs about what you are capable of. If you are an efficiency person, make sure that you identify someone in the team you can trust who isn't and seek their counsel when you need a jolt or some affirmation. Don't allow yourself to be sucked into the myth that the label defines who you are as a leader.

Make sure that you learn how to really monitor your behaviour, so that you can provide choice for your own activities. So often, you see people drowning under the volume of their own actions – sent spiralling by an endless pursuit of efficiency and order. Stress so often begins with a sense of a loss of control, which we reflexively respond to through reactive strategy; it is this that can lead to an efficiency overload and a rapid capsize at the height of the wave.

Productivity: The result of finding the balance

A feeling of equilibrium comes when you find yourself working productively, keeping the balance between the reactive and proactive in check, where efficiency and effectiveness are working together and not in opposition – those days where you still go home knackered but do so feeling a sense of achievement.

Here are a few ideas on just how you can achieve that.

1. Be lean not mean

Beware of weight gain and the impact it can have on your agility. As I get older, believe me I am very aware of that fact, but I'm not talking about pounds and ounces here! As school leaders we live on a diet of new challenges and problems; like cake in the staffroom for a birthday, they demand your attention… immediately. Our reflex is to grab them and deal with them quickly; go too fast, though, and you end up with indigestion and a shock when you step on the scales. In the case of our work, they show themselves as 'to-do' lists, massive ones, bulky and intimidating. In fact, they can become overwhelming.

You've settled down to write a newsletter when an email pings in, followed by a phone call and an urgent request. You start to multitask and, despite common myth, multitasking effectively – no matter your gender – is not possible. You can maybe just about do everything, but you won't do it well, and often you end up creating bigger issues. The newsletter, for example, goes out with a few typos or wrong dates on it and, as we know, there is always one parent or carer waiting in the shadows for just such an occasion. You know the type: the gleeful assassins as I used to call them!

Get into the habit of keeping your lists lean – don't over-schedule, filling your day with too much – so that you can allow for interruption, but make sure that you give yourself time for proactive tasks (PT). I used to go to the gym occasionally, but found that I could only go if I went early in the morning, mainly because if I waited until after work, I was too tired and it was far too easy to procrastinate, avoiding the weights and cardio machine, or at best, haul myself there and end up doing nothing of value because I was simply too exhausted.

Have a master 'to-do' list but break it down each morning into a list for the day ahead. Don't make lists longer than three to five items and make sure you rank them in order of proactive tasks. Do the thing that matters most first: the stuff that really will make a difference, that really fires your sense of leadership and purpose. Don't let the proactive tasks slip down the list; be ruthless, otherwise you will never get there, or if you do, you simply won't have the energy, clarity or capacity to do it justice. It takes real discipline to stay physically lean and the same goes for your lists and actions at school.

Learn to focus on your work and not how long you spend working. For the sake of our collective sanity, we must move on from the belief that how long we work and the amount of our life we sacrifice is equal to our sense of worth or value. There are three known truths about human nature and how we function:

- When our brain is tired, it doesn't work overly well.

- You can't force the generation of ideas; they happen on their own terms. (I find this when I am writing – I used to think writer's block was a myth!)

- When you feel forced to complete something that you know, in that moment, is beyond your capacity, you begin to resent or even hate what you are doing.

Isn't it sad that we do this to our pupils sometimes? Actually, when you think about it, it is as a result of this conditioning that so many of us feel obliged to work in this way, despite these truths.

The discipline to monitor how you feel, so that you don't feel guilty about taking breaks or focusing on something more menial for a while, is vital if we are to move towards real productivity. We must develop in ourselves and in our schools cultures that fight back against measuring how well we work against how long we work; it cannot be about hours but about outcomes.

I used to find it useful at the end of some days to write 'done lists', so that you get into the habit of monitoring what you have *actually* achieved, planned or unplanned. When I write, I have stopped worrying about how many words I've written per day; all that does is create anxiety and the reactions highlighted in the bullet points above. Now I get to it and write until I feel the momentum slow, or a headache coming on. I don't read through what I have written immediately because I always read what I think I have written. Instead I go out for a walk with my dog, come back, review what I've done and stop for the day. I have learnt to measure my efficiency as a writer against the quality of my writing and the degree to which others, hopefully, will find it useful, rather than against the volume of it.

My friend, Richard Gerver, often shares the experience of standing by the photocopier on a Monday morning, listening to colleagues talk about how much of their weekend they gave up to work, in an effort to show how much they care. It is rare to hear them talk about what they actually *did* or of how much value they found it. It is often this same culture that leads to burnout or the growth of professional and personal resentment.

By learning to review what you have actually *achieved* rather than how *hard* you have worked, you can learn how and when you work best and start to take more effective ownership of it.

2. Think positive

This may sound obvious, but we work more effectively when we have a positive attitude. If you can hold onto the value of what you do and remember to look at the real difference you are making to colleagues and students, it helps, because it underlines the significance of what you do, which is an incentive in itself. We are all so easily drawn into the trap of thinking about what we haven't done, what we would or should have done and how we could have done it better that we all too often lose sight of this simple trait. If you feel that what you are doing really makes a positive impact, then you are far more likely to take the initiative and keep looking to work over and above.

As a leader, it is hugely important that you guide your colleagues in the same way. You know whether you're getting the culture right and it's working when staff show a willingness to help a peer in need or offer to pick up something that may be outside their remit. Positive people are also far more likely to take a real pride in what they do. Really significantly, people who are feeling good about what they do are far more likely to trust their instincts and act on their own initiative. As a school leader, the ability to develop a culture of self-leadership is a form of efficiency that allows you to be far more effective and, as a result, gives you time to focus on leading and not managing – being proactive and not reactive.

3. Communication

One of the great strengths of leadership is the ability to communicate but it is amazing how often over the years I saw senior colleagues over-elaborate and therefore complicate what they were trying to say. How many emails have you read, for example, that take a page to say what could have been covered in a sentence? I have often believed that one of the reasons why so many teachers feel so inadequate is the culture of complexity that seems to saturate so much of what we do. I wonder sometimes whether we have become a little like the legal profession, where we have invented a language that we then need to hire people to interpret for us. Effectiveness comes from a commitment to simplicity, and communication must be at the heart of that.

When I have observed really good teachers, what has always struck me is how they take complex concepts and make them so tangible for their students; in many ways, that is the art of great teaching. As leaders we must demand the same of ourselves and those who share leadership with us.

One of the masters of simple language was Apple co-founder Steve Jobs. When he and Apple launched the original iPod®, they were entering an already crowded market in the new digital music age. The difference, though, that made the iPod® an instant success was the way Jobs communicated. Other devices were sold on their technical specifications: memory size, processing speed, sound card capacity, and so on. When Jobs launched the iPod®, he took to the stage in Cupertino and simply said that from tomorrow, '… you can have 4,000 songs in your back pocket'. People got it instantly and so digital music was sold to the masses.

Sometimes we get so tied up, as leaders, in the belief that we need to keep proving ourselves that we increasingly complicate our language in order to show our worth. All that really does, of course, is lead to greater chances of miscommunication, misunderstanding, a lack of buy-in and, ultimately, inefficiency.

Communication is also about *how* we listen. If we are so rushed, so busy and so distracted by the sheer weight of our jobs, we often stop listening effectively and then find ourselves surprised by the reaction from colleagues who become confused and sometimes irritated by our responses. So much of what happens in a school comes from small clues and cues: body language, facial expression and vocal intonation. Most teachers possess good levels of emotional intelligence; we mustn't find ourselves too busy to use it. I can think of many times when, as a head, I was so distracted that when a colleague talked to me about something, I took them too literally and, as a result, ended up escalating the issue by taking the wrong course of action, which of course ends up in even more work.

It is always dangerous if we spend too long in a 'just get it done' mode: where we may think that we are being efficient but actually we are being far from effective. Reading a colleague's situation (such as their early stress about workload, or something happening outside of school such as relationship problems, a poorly relative or a partner who has just lost their job) and then acting upon it may take up time initially, but of course will potentially make a real difference down the line, as well as securing a greater sense of loyalty and trust between you.

4. Routines

One of the great links between efficiency and effectiveness is when we find the discipline to create routines and stick to them. Now, I am a pragmatist and also not a hypocrite; I know, first hand, how hard that can be, especially as a head. It goes back to the example at the start of this chapter. We are, however, creatures of habit and that goes for our brains too. The more of the day-to-day tasks that we can build into a routine, the faster we can get stuff done, because we don't have to think about it. If we get it right, then we have the time and the mental energy to do the really rewarding stuff. It is vital, especially as a non-teaching member of a leadership team, that you create a sense of importance around your routines. As we have discussed, things have changed enormously over the last 30 years in schools. Heads were much more figureheads than CEOs and that meant that they could be found out and about during the school day. Many of us today make the mistake of sacrificing our day to accommodate others; sometimes that is a necessary part of the job but we must ensure that our colleagues respect our timetable as much as we respect theirs. What we do is vital.

5. Automate

For a long time, I wondered why some of the great, creative tech gurus like Steve Jobs wore the same outfit every day. I used to think it was laziness, but it turns out it was more strategic than that. Tony Schwartz, the founder of The Energy Project and co-author of *The Power of Full Engagement* (Loehr and Schwartz, 2003), talks about minimising the need for unnecessary decisions. It turns out that every decision, no matter how small or trivial, can drain your energy. Those moments at Christmas when you walk into the staff room and try to resist a Quality Street or mince pie require energy, and the more you have to consciously regulate your will, the more energy depletes as the day wears on. Good news, I guess: just take the pie and the chocolate for the good of your leadership! I always did and my waistline is paying the price now! Steve Jobs wore the same outfit every day so that he had the energy to think about and act on what *really* mattered. While I am not advocating that we should all go to work every day in blue jeans and a black turtleneck (I think people would comment!), I do think that the ability to audit and 'automate' our thinking as much as possible can make a real difference.

6. Procrastinate

As a school leader and in most aspects of my life, I try to get on top of everything early. As soon as something drops into my in-tray, I try to sort it out – efficiency. It appears, however, that this might not be the best thing to do. Firstly, it creates stress and leads to losing focus. It also means that we end up multitasking, something that neuroscientists are now telling us is a myth. The human brain cannot focus on more than one thing simultaneously; it actually switches between them rapidly. Research evidences that when we do that, we put the brain under considerable strain and therefore we increase energy burn. The good news, therefore, is that procrastination can be a positive thing. Thank goodness, because I can be very good at it! Similarly, giving ourselves lengthy deadlines increases the temptation to multitask and can lead to a lack of effectiveness, so leaving things until almost the last minute sharpens thinking, increases focus and actually turns out to be more efficient. Where you can, try to impose shorter deadlines.

7. Be selfish

Now I know that as an educator, this is somewhat counter-intuitive but… We chose to work in education because we love teaching and working with pupils. All too often, we get so tied up in surviving the job that we lose sight of the joy. As I've mentioned previously, as a head, I used to love taking assembly; I had the chance to vent my drama and storytelling skills, working with the children. It would often set me up for the day. The energy I got from working with my pupils is something I still miss dreadfully. I used to love going on school trips and residentials, or teaching, even on a wet Thursday afternoon. Where you can, be selfish and make time every week to do what you love: being a teacher. Yes, you could have been writing that head's report or signing off a risk assessment, but it can wait and the recharge you get from doing a little of what you love means that you will be far more efficient in the long run.

Summary

- Remind yourself of the early days of your leadership. Reflect on what worked and why. Find time to bring back some of those strategies.
- Find a colleague, either inside your school or a peer you know and trust from elsewhere, and make time for a chat by putting dates in your diary. Reflect and share with no set agenda.
- Make sure that you work on at least one proactive task every day.
- Audit the decisions you take and see where you can automate them and reduce energy burn.
- Insist on simple communication.
- Take time to be a teacher. Block time every week to spend with the pupils.

8 Control and empowerment

True leaders don't create followers, they create more leaders.

Tom Peters

I will be honest with you and say that I do like to be in control of things. I like to know what my diary looks like for the following week. If somebody is going to call in, I want to know when. When someone says they'll give me a lift, I will ask them what time they will come. I know that I am getting worse as I get older, but I can't change the way that I am (or perhaps it is more that I don't want to).

When I left headship after 15 years in order to write my first book, *Leading from the Edge* (a book so honest – and hopefully thought-provoking and helpful – that I could not write it while still in post), I gave up most semblances of routine. There was no monthly salary coming in and, to begin with, my diary looked pretty empty. These days, thankfully, it is rather fuller with speaking commitments, and I am still writing of course. However, I still never know when the phone might ring, or somebody might enquire about a keynote at a conference or a staff training day. That is all beyond my control and I guess over time I have got used to it. Don't get me wrong; I love what I do but it can be a little unpredictable at times and so I try to control the things that I can. The more in control I feel over my life, the happier I am.

I am sure that I am not alone in this. As we will see in the next chapter, cynicism is often borne out of a sense of powerlessness – that nothing we can do will change things so why bother? It is what Dr Martin Seligman (2018), one of the pioneers of positive psychology, refers to as 'learned helplessness'.

Time to reflect

Think of a time in your career when you felt particularly happy and fulfilled.

- How in control did you feel of your destiny on a scale of 1 to 10 (with 10 being high)?

Now think of a point in your career when you felt unfulfilled and/or unhappy.

- How in control did you feel of your destiny on a scale of 1 to 10 (with 10 being high)?

Feeling powerful – literally feeling 'able' – comes from a deep sense of being in control of life.

Kouzes and Posner (2017)

There is then a clear link in my mind between how much we enjoy the role of leader and how much we feel in control of our own destiny.

So, control is a good thing, right?

Well yes and no. (There's nothing like sitting on the fence!) 'Feeling in control' is a phrase that has positive connotations. 'Being controlling' is a phrase that has very negative connotations, both in terms of personal relationships and also as a trait in those who seek to lead others.

In one manner or another, we all seek a degree of control in our leadership lives. Without it we consign ourselves to being constantly buffeted by the waves, with no wind in our sails and completely at the mercy of outside influences. Our leadership journey will be perilous and, most likely, short-lived.

It is a question of moderation, as indeed applies to most things in life. Broadly speaking, a school leader's control can be broken down into two areas, **internal** and **external** control.

Internal control

This is where control can almost certainly be considered to be a good thing. Leaders who regularly fail to consider their own wellbeing or to achieve a high degree of self-control often don't just buckle or snap, but find themselves falling into bad habits and destructive behaviours such as alcohol or other substance abuse (more common than you might think), or gambling, leading to problems in their personal lives, which often then spill over into their world of work. It's a slippery slope and one that generally does not end well. As well as a good degree of self-awareness and self-regulation, school leaders need to master three areas of internal control.

1. Attitude

In order to move any year group, department or school forward, you need to have maximum impact through your words and actions. In times of worry, confusion and particularly in times of change (which few people enjoy), people are looking to you for reassurance. They want to believe that *you* believe that things will be OK. Unpick the emotions you are feeling yourself. If they are positive ones, look for ways to amplify them and share them with staff. If, on the other hand, they are negative, that's OK (no one is positive the whole time – if they say they are, they are either deluding themselves or lying!) but look for ways to minimise those feelings.

2. Reactions

I did not always get this right I have to admit, but you have to learn to respond to situations (and people!) rather than react to them. Give yourself, at the very least, a few seconds to consider all sides and points of view or you will, sometimes, say things that you come to regret. As I used to say to my Year 6s when they fell out, 'Once you have said something, you cannot unsay it.' I think it was my grandma who taught me that particular lesson in life. What she did not go on to teach me, but I learned in leadership, is that body language and facial expressions can be equally as damaging. The closed-language arm-fold, the scowl or dismissive rolling of the eyes can be every bit as damaging to relationships as any words that may be spoken. As a leader you need to be in control of your emotional and physical reactions in every situation.

3. Personality bias

It is human nature that we get on with some people better than others. For the most part I can rub along well with most people, but it would be fair to say that there have been one or two members of staff that I have struggled to get on with. (The most obvious of these was Joanne, a very local member of staff, who I brought onto the senior leadership team on the basis that it was better to have the camel on the inside pi**ing out than on the outside pi**ing in. Big mistake: she leaked like a sieve!) On the other hand, there were members of staff I really connected with. These were generally the people who did not take the day off at the drop of a hat like Mrs bloody Jones. Only in the most exceptional of circumstances did they bring their domestic dramas to work with them. They worked hard but did not whinge about it. They did not gossip about others and if they did from time to time disagree with you, they were able to do so in a mature fashion and without lasting resentment. Come on, who would not like members of staff like that? Of course I had my favourites! Don't we all?

Of course we are never able to publicly admit it and we must never ignore the golden rule, which is that while we may privately have our favourites, it does not give us licence to treat them any better or to ignore other members of our team, who are equally entitled to our time.

External control

This essentially is the need to have control over factors *outside* ourselves in order to achieve a desired set of outcomes. This, one would hope, would include such aims as improving the life chances of pupils, a happy and fulfilled workforce and a school that is central to and serves its community. However, and perhaps inevitably, given the current educational climate, the focus can become about achieving a particular set of test or exam results or a sought-after inspection grading. While many leaders do achieve a balance between these drivers (despite often very challenging circumstances), some leaders do become obsessive about 'the scores on the doors'. It is not a place that any one of us set out to be in when we entered school leadership, but it is where some leaders find themselves, for a wide variety of reasons. If that obsession does take hold, leaders can succumb to high levels of controlling behaviour towards staff, abuse of power, coercion and sometimes cheating in order to achieve the sense of feeling in control that they crave. I know of a headteacher who, on the day before inspection and parent questionnaires went online, got his staff to open the incoming responses and dispose of most of the negative ones, replacing them with forged positive ones. Another head I know of, in the early days of Key Stage 2 SATs (when checks on the opening of papers did not exist), sent home the entire contents of the spelling paper as 'this week's spelling homework'. It is amazing what a (thankfully) very small number of leaders will resort to in order to achieve a sense of control.

The command and control model

One of the most common approaches to leadership in industry, commerce and particularly the military is the notion of the leader as commander and controller: the person at the 'top of the pile' directing those beneath. Such leaders have ten common behaviour traits:

1 They expend energy promoting themselves as leader and figurehead, rather than sharing credit and exposure with the team.

2 They give directions and orders rather than asking questions or listening to others.

3 They treat staff as subordinates as opposed to colleagues.

4 They make decisions quickly and generally without consulting others.

5 They place results above people.

6 They despise failure rather than seeing it as part of the learning process.

7 They build teams that carry out their instructions rather than ones with the creative power to innovate.

8 They can't abide dissent and close down constructive criticism.

9 They place a low priority on innovation, ideas and fun in the workplace, believing that these get in the way of productivity.

10 They instruct rather than empower.

Motivations for a command and control approach

The term 'control freak' is used widely and not as a term of endearment, I might add! If you have been lucky enough to avoid working for a boss who is a bit of a control freak, then well done. To be fair, I have only worked for one and it was very early on in my career, but I have met a few others along the way. I have often wondered what made them tick. What had happened in their life and professional back story that made them into the school leaders they became?

Now, I am not a psychologist, but I have read quite a lot and written a bit now about human behaviour, so this is my personal attempt to explain it.

This is my pen portrait of Mr Logan. (This is a name I have chanced upon by looking up from my laptop and seeking inspiration from books and DVDs around my office. My eyes fell upon a DVD called *Logan* starring Hugh Jackman – a film I have yet to watch and will probably not get to watch until I have completed this book!)

Mr Logan has a clear view of the world in general and education in particular (nothing unusual in that). He has a need to feel valued (don't we all?). In order to feel valued, he must firstly survive and secondly be seen as successful. But this is where he starts to veer away from other leaders because Mr Logan has a fairly narrow definition of what success means. He sees life's events in black and white terms, i.e. you either win or you lose. If you lose you are not successful and therefore you will not be valued. Losing indicates weakness and, just as in any David Attenborough programme you have ever watched on the BBC, weakness makes you vulnerable to attack by those who might want to dethrone you and take your place. Mr Logan loathes the thought of being vulnerable.

Mr Logan – let's humanise him by giving him a first name: Robert (Robert Downey Jr. – still not got round to *Avengers: Endgame* either!) – needs to feel safe and the best way for that to happen is by getting things done, either doing them himself or by getting other people to do them for him. Much as he would like to do everything himself, he recognises that in a school that is not possible. He cannot teach every lesson in every class in every year group, so he does at least recognise that he needs other people in that respect.

The difficulty that Robert now has is that he doesn't just want things done. He wants them done perfectly. Perfection is another marker of success and success makes him feel safe and that is why controlling leaders are addicted to perfection. They crave safety.

Rob's view of perfection (we can call him by his shortened name as we are getting to know him quite well now) is based, though, on how *he* would do things and sadly few will ever meet that standard, though he will never tire of trying to make them through the art of micromanagement.

When Rob gets things done he feels safe and good about himself, and so taking charge of every situation and imposing his will on his staff becomes his default style of leadership.

Unfortunately, his lack of trust leaves Rob feeling isolated and more than a little paranoid. He gets over this by imposing his will even further to make him feel safe.

OK, a little extreme, or perhaps not? It depends on your career experiences to date.

Time to reflect

Have you ever known a leader like Robert, or a Roberta? If not an exact match, someone who displays some of those tendencies?

Can you think of an example of that control and command behaviour?

What happened?

How did you feel yourself?

How did it impact on other members of the team?

What would you do differently?

The drawbacks of command and control

A controlling style of leadership can be very effective when there is need for a rapid transformational change in schools, but when it becomes the standard mode of operation over a long period of time then the drawbacks become more noticeable. Among them are:

1   It is based on the assumption that the leader always knows best, which is rarely the case in my experience.

2   Staff will rarely apply maximum effort to any plan that they do not buy into unless it is out of fear, which makes for a really unhealthy atmosphere in school. You can soon sense it if you visit such a school.

3   In an effort to be seen to be making progress quickly, leaders can be tempted to embark on transformational change before they have crystallised their thinking on what they want the outcomes to look like. (Sounds a little like UK politics...)

The above can cause leaders to have to make U-turns or at least partial course corrections, which can damage credibility and fuel cynicism. Being told exactly how to do your job limits the engagement of staff as well as the discretionary effort they are willing to put in, destroying the goodwill that is the currency that schools are built on and actually promoting resistance.

Direction vs control

Now I guess that when you look back at those traits of controlling leaders I listed above, they do not seem particularly attractive as a package. I do not recognise it as an entity that would sum up my time in 23 years in school leadership and

I hope that anyone who worked with me would not see me in that list. I also guess that you are not, and would not aspire to be, that kind of a leader either. (If you did, you would not have made it this far through the book!) However, before we dismiss it as a leadership model that is not appropriate for schools, let's think about it from another angle.

Different schools need different leadership styles in different times and effective leaders need a wide variety of tools in their toolbox. To use our sailing analogy, the way you would prepare to set sail when you are in an unfamiliar boat with a crew you have not worked with before would be very different from a boat and crew you have worked with many times before. With a new boat and crew, you would need to establish your authority as skipper, make clear the course you are going to be sailing and what your expectations are of the crew – who should be doing what and when – otherwise chaos! To helm the boat in these initial times in your relationship, you would need to employ *some* of those characteristics from the list above and so it is when you take up a new leadership role. Staff need to know your direction of travel and your expectations – otherwise, here too, chaos!

In these circumstances, it would be more appropriate to call this style of leadership 'directive' rather than command and control. One of the things that **Patrick Ottley-O'Connor** has impressed upon me is this need to adapt your style of leadership over time. Bearing in mind that Patrick usually works as executive head at a school for one year only, his style of leadership changes as the ship turns and sails off on the course that he is setting. 'At first it is visionary (you need a clear vision and then get people on board to help), then pace-setting and directive with clear non-negotiables, e.g. no mobile phones.' Once there is a clarity of purpose and expectation then things 'become more affiliative as time goes on with a move towards coaching by the first half term. You might speak to and listen to people more, but you still end up making the decisions. You are paid to make the decisions.'

Empowerment

The long-term solution to transformation change lies in empowerment. It is a word much used in modern parlance but, a bit like the word 'stress', it means different things to different people.

The *Collins English Dictionary* describes it as a noun, meaning 'the process of giving [a person or group of people] power and status in a particular situation'.

Or on that most reliable of sources, Wikipedia, empowerment refers to 'measures designed to increase the degree of autonomy and self-determination in people and in communities in order to enable them to represent their interests in a responsible and self-determined way, acting on their own authority'.

Actually, I feel myself quite drawn to the Wikipedia definition. Using that definition then, and applying the general rule that the more in control we feel, the happier we are, there is a close link between feeling empowered and feeling content. History teaches us that discontent among the workforce is rarely a good thing.

The advantages of empowerment in school leadership

The climate is right… You have left harbour and plotted your course. You have briefed your crew, whatever the role, on your direction of travel and your expectations. You have enthused them. You have energised them. You have engaged them. Great adventures (and some waves) lie ahead. So, what next?

- **Vision:** You have set out the course you are setting off on, your mission and why you are doing it.
- **Enthuse:** You have got people to see the brighter dawn – that things can and will be better.
- **Energise:** You have given them that all-important self-belief that is the foundation of excitement.
- **Engage:** From cleaner to midday supervisor and teaching assistant, from teacher to school business manager, they all know that they have a role to play in making the vision come to life.
- **EMPOWERMENT.**

Built-in empowerment

Most teachers come already empowered. It is like the pre-installed software on my new iPhone®: there are many apps already there at my disposal. I like it a lot, but I am really struggling with facial recognition software as opposed to a keycode to get in. (It does not seem to recognise me if I am wearing glasses, which increasingly I need to do. Nor does it seem to have a clue who I am if I am wearing a woolly hat, which, as it is winter at present, I am quite a lot!) Consequently, because I don't want it or understand it (or perhaps I am a little frightened of it), I am looking for ways to turn the damn thing off – the facial recognition software, that is, not the phone itself.

Some leaders do this with their staff. The vast majority of teachers enter the profession thinking that they can make a difference to children's lives. They have a 'can-do' attitude and have a sense of personal efficacy that drives them to do whatever they need to do (within the law of course) to make a difference. However, not all leaders want this. They want regulation and uniformity and teachers who are, well, like them, or at the very least are prepared to do their bidding. The new and exciting software that the teacher has to offer gets switched off, extinguished.

There are three major problems with this.

Firstly, it is the 'can-do' attitude that sustains staff's beliefs and their efforts when the waves come crashing down, which they will do from time to time.

Secondly, it is by putting people in charge and in control of their professional lives that we grow school leaders of the future. People with no self-belief and without the ability to explore and learn from their mistakes without fear of the wrath of their leaders do not have the opportunity to grow. Not the ideal climate for propagating the next generation of school leaders that our education system so desperately needs.

Thirdly, as Kouzes and Posner (2017) put it: 'Organisational effectiveness depends upon the sharing or distribution, not the hoarding, of power and influence.' They go on to relay a quote from the late American, Major General John Stanford, who once said, 'We don't get our power from our stars and bars. We get our power from the people we lead.'

How true.

When I look back over my career as a teacher, the times I felt most **enthusiastic**, **energised**, **engaged** and, yes, **empowered** were when I worked with school leaders who:

- gave me choices
- encouraged self-leadership
- helped me to develop my skills and knowledge
- held me to account.

I had not really thought about it until now, but yes, that is what they all had in common.

Empowerment and accountability

With empowerment **must** come accountability. Without it, well, chaos!

If there are no expectations and consequences, sadly there will always be some people in the staffroom who will just not care. You would not want to set to sea in a boat where one of the crew just didn't care. While you do not need to watch them carry out every last manoeuvre, you *would* want to know that if a course correction is required they would actually do it. Secondly, once other members of the crew notice that person does not care and, more importantly, is getting away with it, they will gradually stop caring too. The ship goes down. I have witnessed it happen.

In the months before I had become a substantive head, I was seconded as acting head for two terms in a small village primary school that had recently gone into special measures. The head had been told by the local authority what she could expect over the coming months and what would be required, and, as is often the case, she had decided to take early retirement.

There were six classes and around eight teachers, when you took into account job shares. The head herself taught for four days a week. I take my hat off to teaching heads; I only did it for a short period of time and it almost brought me to my knees. What had evolved was a system, if you can call it that, of high empowerment and no accountability, with teachers free to teach pretty much whatever they wanted as there were no planned schemes of work to speak of. Some teachers had not been observed for years and there were accusations of bullying by one male member of staff that had been swept under the carpet.

It was bedlam and trying to put into place structures and accountability in the free-for-all was one of the toughest challenges of my career. The poorest teachers were employing teaching techniques that would not have been out of place in Dickens's *Bleak House*. Those in that camp resisted any accountability, or 'interference' as they saw it. On the other hand, the good teachers actually welcomed the accountability and were pleased that someone was showing interest in their work.

I would like to think that I left the school in a better place than I found it.

A cautionary note on accountability

Handled badly, accountability *can* come back to bite you as a leader, for two main reasons.

Firstly, it only really works if a member of staff *knows* up front that they are going to be held to account for their performance. This gives them an opportunity to modify their actions and behaviour if required. To be told after an event denies them the opportunity to do so. To withhold any reward or impose any sanction in relation to performance management would be perceived as unfair. That's because it is!

Secondly, staff must believe and trust that the methods for tracking and assessing their performance are both accurate and fair. It stands to reason, doesn't it? Think of it from your own position. If someone is going to hold you to account for your actions, and there are going to be consequences, either good or bad, you would want to be pretty clear what they are expecting of you. You would also want to know that, come the time of reckoning, your performance will be measured purely on those expectations, because anything else would be unfair.

And that's the point. We all need accountability, but it will only work if it is clear, transparent and fair.

Ten tips for empowering your staff

1. **Share your vision.** Do it regularly and in straightforward language. Communicate well and often; otherwise staff will fill in the gaps for themselves.

2. **Be approachable.** You cannot empower staff if they are too frightened to even talk to you.

3. **Build relationships.** Empowerment relies on developing staff. You can only do that if you know them.

4. **Help staff to see their value and purpose.** Help them to see your vision for your school, department, or year group and the important contribution that they can make.

5. **Develop staff.** Budgets are tight but look for low-cost methods such as focused class swaps. They need to know their career development matters to you.

6. **Involve staff in decisions.** You cannot do this all the time, but where you can, do. They will feel listened to and involved.

7. **Recognise people's efforts and success in public.** They should never go unrecognised and it encourages discretionary effort.

8. **Correct staff in private.** Public correction is both humiliating and will lead to feelings of disempowerment.

9. **Encourage a culture where mistakes and failures are seen as learning opportunities.** A developing school needs innovation and

Control and empowerment

innovation requires risk. Staff are more likely to have a go if they do not fear being torn down.

10 **Don't micromanage.** Give your staff the freedom to work creatively and develop their own ideas without someone watching over their shoulder the whole time.

Summary

- There is a distinct difference between 'being in control' as a leader and being 'controlling'.
- Internal control encompasses **attitude**, **reactions** and **personality bias**.
- External control often manifests itself in either **command** or **empowerment**.
- **Command** and **control** are based on the assumption that the leader always knows best.
- Different schools need different leadership styles at different stages of their journey.
- Empowerment is the long-term key to transformational change in schools.
- **Vision**, **enthuse**, **energise** and **engage** are all necessary steps before **empowerment** can really happen.
- It is by putting people in charge and in control of their professional lives that we are able to grow the leaders of the future.
- For schools to develop, leaders need to share and distribute power rather than hoard it.
- Empowerment should be accompanied by systems of accountability that are both transparent and fair.

---

9 Avoiding the creep of cynicism

I don't believe that things always happen for the best, but I do believe that it's possible to make the best of things that happen.

Tal Ben-Shahar and Angus Ridgway (2017)

It's 1998. Robbie Williams is riding high in the UK charts with 'Angels', along with All Saints' 'Never Ever' and Boyzone's 'No Matter What'. (Most) European nations agree on a single currency, the Euro, and *Harry Potter and the Chamber of Secrets* (the book) has come out.

Amid these seismic events, a relatively young James Hilton attended his first local authority headteachers' meeting. The local authority was still very influential back then, so most heads were in attendance. I didn't really know anyone in the room, at least not enough to ask if I could join their small clusters in one of the rows of theatre-style seating. Where to sit? Certainly not the front row; I would look very much the newbie and too eager to please. Back row? Might look a little uninterested and that would not go down well. Eventually, I plumped for a seat next to the centre aisle about a third of the way back. Sitting in front of me were a man and a woman who, I found out later, were husband and wife headteachers of two different schools.

The meeting was being led by a local authority adviser called David. Now, I quite liked David. He seemed to talk a lot of sense and he had been involved in the selection panel for my new job. Assuming all indicators, he had probably been happy with my appointment, so not only did he talk a lot of sense, but he was also a man of exquisite taste and good judgement!

I cannot remember any of the agenda of that meeting, partly because it was a very long time ago, but mainly because I became increasingly transfixed by the married heads in front of me. Let's call them Heather and Tony because those were their names. (No, only kidding, I am not so stupid as to invite a libel case – I have seen too many episodes of *Have I Got News for You*.) Every time David announced any piece of news or policy initiative, they would nudge one another with their elbows. This was usually accompanied by turning to one another and rolling their eyes or staring at one another meaningfully. They were clearly of the 'seen it all before and it didn't work then, and it won't work now' variety of school leaders.

I didn't want any part of it and avoided them like the plague at all subsequent meetings. I can remember thinking that if I ever ended up as cynical as them, I hoped that someone would shoot me to put me out of my misery, rather as they do a horse. I swore that I would never end up like them. Thirty years on and I am proud to say that I am still here, relatively intact, although I have endured a few flesh wounds along the way!

I don't suppose Heather and Tony set out to become the cynics that they were. Few join the profession for the holidays or the salary and if they do, they don't tend to hang around long. Most of us sign up because we want to make a difference to the next generation and the impact that they will have on the world in which they will grow up.

There is a little bit of Heather and Tony in all of us, I think. There is not one single point at which we think, 'Oh, I am going to become cynical now', but like driftwood washed up by waves on the shore, some leaders end up in a place where they swore that they would never be.

Why do leaders become cynical?

A combination of factors, I would suggest, but I think it boils down to this: the longer you are a school leader, the more you have seen and the more knocks you will have taken.

I have lost count of the number of Secretaries of State for Education I have seen through. All desperate to make their mark on education, making rushed decisions that were not thought through in the hope that they will not have to see them through because they will have been promoted to some other higher-profile cabinet position by then. Travel back in time and you will find a much younger (slimmer and with more hair too) version of me sending an ironic Christmas card to the then Secretary of State for Education, Kenneth Baker, the 'inventor' of the INSET day or 'Baker Days' as they were known back then. So many Secretaries of State, so many broken promises (on all sides of the political divide) – it is enough to make anyone a little bit cynical. Please, somebody slap me now because I can feel myself getting sucked into the cynic in me even as I write (gentle slaps only please; I don't need my jaw breaking here).

Most of us enter into school leadership in the hope that our paths will largely be unobstructed. In other words, we know that there will be waves but we hope that they will not be too big. You simply see more over time. The more you see, the more you know: the heartbreaks, the politics and the people whom you thought you could trust but who ultimately let you down. All these things can, if you let them, become the perfect incubator for cynicism.

The basis of cynicism is often a sense of powerlessness: the feeling as a leader that the odds are completely stacked against you. You don't need me to tell you that these are tough times in education. Budgets have shrunk to a point where schools are appealing to parents for financial help with the very basics. My last school has lost a raft of teaching assistants and that is far from an unusual picture.

Compounded with this is the lasting sense that politicians with an education brief are rather more in it for their own political gain than for the benefit of the pupils that we are desperate to serve and give the best chance in life. They introduce a new initiative to make a quick impact and then move on, leaving school leaders to pick up the pieces. It is not a new phenomenon.

School leaders often find themselves caught between what is being asked of them from those above and the needs of their pupils.

And then there is the farce of UK and world politics. If you had pitched it as a script for a TV show ten years ago, people would have called it fanciful.

And then there is climate change…

Listen to me… I sound so cynical. I really am not by nature, but it is so easy to get drawn in.

Once we get caught in this spiral, we can also project cynicism into new situations. For example, any new policy initiative that seems vaguely familiar can evoke a response of 'It did not work then and it won't work now!' I used to teach alongside Roger (again, name changed), who was just like that, and it would be fair to say he sapped the life right out of me – nice guy but he had no interest or curiosity in how things could be improved for the children that we taught. The curious school leaders are never cynical. Cynics will never change the world of education but will rather tell you that it will never change, or if it does, it will only be for the worse.

Time to reflect

Have you encountered the Rogers of this world?

How did they make you feel?

What was the impact of their outlook on life for the students?

What did you do to ameliorate their impact?

In defence of cynicism

Up to a point, cynicism gets itself a bad name. After all, I can't think of many people who would genuinely look to be described as being cynical. It is not the most attractive of personality traits, and yet, if on trial, there is a case for our inner cynic.

Imagine that you are lying on a sun lounger on the beach in some tropical paradise. Working the sun worshippers is a salesman. He approaches you and offers to sell you a 'genuine' Rolex watch for the equivalent of £100. Even after three Malibu and cokes (the worst hangover I ever had was drinking that combo – I still can't look a coconut in the eye, but that's a tale for another time!), you would be a little bit cynical, wouldn't you? I know I would be. Particularly when I notice that it says 'Rollex' rather than 'Rolex' in very small print on the dial.

Or, imagine that a new parent governor, who runs a business offering before- and after-school care, wants to make a significant cash donation to your school. Mmm – ulterior motive? (And a true story!)

In measured amounts, cynicism helps to keep us from harm. It is part of our self-preservation instinct, protecting us from the waves of knockbacks and disappointments that will inevitably come our way over time.

To be continued…

…

…

…

…

…

…

So why the gap, you ask?

Well, I will tell you honestly that my mother passed away during the writing of this chapter. I am not going for sympathy here. Her name was Pat. She was 88, so from that point of view, it was not entirely unexpected, but she had not really been unwell, so from another angle it was a bit of a shock. She did not suffer, and my brother was with her when she died in her own home, so that was a blessing. Needless to say, it has blown me a little off course and I have not written anything for two months now. Partly because I just haven't been 'in the zone' and partly because of holidays and speaking commitments. (Hannah, my editor, has had the patience of a saint. Thank you!) However, I am back and determined to crack on (hopefully you will be pleased at that prospect if you have made it this far through the book!).

However, what I have learned from the experience is that sometimes we all need to take a bit of a step back to pause and reflect if we are going to continue successfully on our journey – a chance to recharge the batteries. More on this in the next chapter on page 155.

More on this in the next chapter on page 155.

Back to the plot… So where were we?

While resisting the needless shove of endless policy initiatives from above may be popular with staff, being a cynic is absolutely not!

I have read many leadership books over the years but have yet to read one that extols cynicism as a virtue. Cynicism is based on the belief that everybody is purely in it for themselves. An extension of this is mistrust. While I have mistrusted the sincerity and intentions of some people above me over the years, I would like to think I had trust in the intentions of the staff I worked with. One or two, inevitably, let me down over the years, but I would always start from a position of trust.

In essence, being cynical with your staff is tantamount to leadership suicide. It breeds a culture of mistrust and that is no basis on which to build any kind of organisation, let alone a school.

Cynicism is a self-imposed blindness, a rejection of the world because we are afraid it will hurt us or disappoint us.

Stephen Colbert

As **Angela Browne** said to me in conversation for this book, 'Initiative overload contributes hugely to cynicism, but it is only an issue if you take on every initiative. You have to be brave enough to decide which ones you are going to take on. It's about hearts and minds. Which initiatives are going to help us get to where we want to be?'

At the heart of all this there are three simple messages:

- **We owe it to staff to remain positive.** Whatever waves come crashing down on us, staff will look to their leaders for comfort, reassurance and hope.

- **We owe it to our students.** To paraphrase something that **Hannah Wilson** said to me a few months back, 'The day we cannot look a five-year-old child in the eye and be optimistic about their future is probably the time we should give up.'

- **We owe it to ourselves.** Once cynicism gets a hold on you and you become mistrustful of colleagues, their abilities and motivations, you rapidly become isolated. You end up going it alone and, as I always say, isolation is the biggest enemy of resilience. An isolated leader may not always see it, but they eventually become far more mentally vulnerable and, because constantly having to rely on your own inner resources is exhausting, they are at far greater risk of burnout. For some it may take months, for others it may take many years, but going it alone eventually takes its toll.

When was the last time you felt professionally cynical?

What were the circumstances?

Can you trace it back to past events that may have been the trigger for those cynical feelings? Was a promise to you broken? Were you criticised unfairly?

Ten ways to avoid cynicism clouding your leadership judgement

It is very easy as a leader to become cynical and there is so much out there to fuel that cynicism, and yet, in our heart of hearts we know it is the wrong path. We deal in the futures of young people and we have a duty to remain optimistic, if not for ourselves, then for them. Cynicism is the path to the dark side of the force. (Forgive me, I am going to see the concluding chapter of *Star Wars* tomorrow and I am as excited as I was when I went to see the original back in 1977 at the age of 14 – damn, now you know my exact age!) None of us want to go down that path but how do we avoid it? I am channelling my inner Yoda here as I provide some suggestions.

1. Analyse the basis of your cynicism

Our cynicism is often a gut instinct reaction to a person, situation or set of circumstances. As such we tend to focus on the present and our current feelings. However, if we can trace back, as in the exercise above, to how previous events have led us to be mistrustful of our current circumstances, we can start to project forward more positive outcomes to our present dilemma, i.e. just because something has happened to us in the past, it doesn't mean it will happen again. No two sets of circumstances are exactly the same. Much of anxiety, fear or hatred is illogical. If you write things down and debate the issue with yourself or someone you trust, it often becomes clear how illogical some of those thoughts are, reducing the potency of those emotions.

2. Take a step back

Give yourself some space and try to look at the source of your cynicism objectively. Is it part of a consistent pattern of behaviour on the part of the perceived perpetrator, or is it a one-off event? Does the situation have a lasting impact or merely a fleeting one? Does it truly breech your core principles or is it actually more of an annoyance?

3. Try to forgive

Negative events stick with us for a very long time and can cast a long shadow. Most people, depending on their age, can tell you exactly where they were when they learned of the attack on the Twin Towers or when Diana, Princess of Wales, was killed in a road tunnel in Paris while being harassed by the paparazzi. I suspect that the same will be true of the Grenfell Tower disaster in years to come.

You will have led a charmed professional life if all your experiences have been positive and if you reach retirement age without experiencing the feeling that someone has let you down or even stabbed you in the back.

I remember being in my final year of primary school and the school was fundraising for the RSPCA.

One lunchtime, my friend Andrew and I were running a raffle in the school entrance hall while our classmates Deborah and Caroline were running some other kind of stall, I don't remember what, on the other side of the space. What I do remember, though, is that Andrew and I were doing rather well, and business was brisk. Lord Sugar would have been proud of our patter and flare, I like to think. Deborah and Caroline were doing less well, and I can't deny there was a little bit of crowing going on on our part.

At some point, Deborah cracked and ran across the entrance hall and grabbed a handful of our hard-earned cash and quickly dashed back to her stall to boost their coffers. Crying foul, I sprinted across the open space and grabbed a handful of coins to redress the balance. The raid and the accompanying shrieks from Deborah and Caroline were witnessed by Mr Killdon, the deputy head.

Unwilling to listen to any explanation on my part, it was instant dismissal from my post. To make it worse, he also sacked me from my post as custard monitor in the dining hall the following week (there was no such thing as health and safety back then so no one batted an eyelid at the thought of a ten-year-old liberally dispensing scalding hot liquid – simpler times!).

As these events happened over *40* years ago (quite a bit over 40 years ago) and I can clearly recall them when I have forgotten most of the lessons I was ever taught back then, you will see that I have had a tough time forgiving Mr Killdon. The man clearly hated me and was out to find any reason at all to punish me for some trumped-up misdemeanour. He was quite clearly an evil *megalomaniac*! I stopped sending him Christmas cards as punishment. Hah! I bet that hurt him.

When someone lets us down or seems to betray our trust, we have a tendency to judge not only their behaviour, but also the motives behind their behaviour. We often cast them as the pantomime villain who at no point meant to treat us fairly. Psychologists refer to this tendency as the fundamental attribution error.

Klein and Epley (2017) suggest that we tend to be a little easier on ourselves. We may make mistakes, but we *know* our intentions and we *meant* well and therefore we generally forgive ourselves more quickly.

Given that cynicism is often borne out of hurt and pain, the more we are able to 'park' and move on from an issue, the more we are able to stop it from fuelling our cynicism. Not easy I know at times, but resentment is like holding a glass of water in your outstretched hand. A glass of water is not heavy, but hold onto it long enough and it will most certainly start to weigh you down. Small acts of kindness towards the person you resent can certainly help you to let go.

Mr Killdon, you are forgiven.

4. Exercise your sense of curiosity

The seed of optimism has to be curiosity. Rather than judging what you believe you have already learned, try something new. Explore a new interest, perspective or possibility, in either your professional or personal life. Opening yourself to new possibilities and opportunities keeps cynicism at bay. Be a lifelong learner. There is a whole chapter on curiosity in my book *Leading from the Edge* if you want to explore this further.

5. Avoid catastrophising and challenge your assumptions

It is easy to slip into the mindset of anticipating and projecting the worst possible outcomes to any situation. When we do so, we often end up in a spiral of negative self-talk, and the more time we spend chewing on those negative thoughts, the more powerful they become until they threaten to engulf us.

I used to get very wound up if I knew a parent had booked an appointment to come and see me and I did not know why. The longer the lead-in to the meeting, the longer I had to imagine the reasons behind it. A bullying incident? A complaint about a member of staff? Ruminating on it could distract me from what I really needed to be getting on with, but in all honesty, in 23 years of school leadership, how often were those meetings as bad as I had imagined? I could probably count them on one hand. Challenge your assumptions.

6. Look for the positives

Most clouds have some sort of silver lining; try to find it.

For instance, the windows of the school in my first headship were very insecure and comparatively easy to open, by sliding a thin metal object such as a table knife into the gap between window and frame (genius design!). I think this was widely known in the neighbourhood. Consequently, if the site manager was unavailable for any reason, I was next on the call-out list. On one occasion, I had to make the 30-mile round trip at around 11 pm. The intruders had gained entry through a classroom window and pretty much ransacked the staffroom, main office and my office. It was, frankly, a massive pain in the neck, to put it politely but… anyone who ever worked with me will know my office was often a bit of a bombsite. I knew where everything was because everything was filed either under 'D' for desk, 'W' for windowsill or 'F' for floor. It was fine, unless anybody else had to find things in my absence. The silver lining of the break-in was that it finally gave me the impetus to declutter and clear out all the folders and paperwork I had hung onto 'just in case….'

Finding that silver lining can help us not to see events as inherently negative and prevent the onset of cynicism.

7. Choose who you spend your time with

Jim Rohn (2012), a famous motivational speaker, once said, 'You are the average of the five people you spend your time with.'

Just as schools eventually become like their leaders, leaders themselves eventually become like the people they spend their time with. Now, I am not suggesting you employ staff 'in your own image'. That rarely goes well. We all need people to challenge our thinking from time to time and you will only find an oyster in the shell if there has been a piece of grit in there too.

Rather, I am suggesting that when you go to meetings you avoid the Heathers and the Tonys of this world. World-weary cynicism is highly contagious in education, but the good news is that so is positivity, but you have to be in close proximity to someone to catch either one.

8. Take yourself outside and give yourself a good talking to

We all like a bit of a moan and a grumble from time to time but if you spend much of your time doing this in front of your colleagues, you are not leading them. Serial complainers become situation-focused and often find it difficult to move outside of the constraints of the current problem. Effective school leaders are solution-focused, which is far more energising for all concerned. They work with their team to identify problems and look for ways to solve them for the benefit of the whole school community. They do not make issues personal. Good leaders do not attack people; they focus their energy on attacking problems.

9. Control the controllable

Cynicism, as we have established, is borne out of a sense of a powerlessness and yet we are rarely completely powerless in any situation. If I had a potentially volatile meeting with staff, parents or governors, I would remind myself that the meeting was taking place on my turf, my manor, as I am sure they would say on *EastEnders*. As such, while I could not control the overall arc of the meeting, there were things I *could* control, such as how I stood, who sat where and on what sized chair (all power games I know but often very, very effective), and what would be the content and tone of my opening remarks. My turf, my meeting, so I will speak first.

Working hard to reduce our feelings of powerlessness in any situation is empowering, reducing feelings of negativity and cynicism.

10. Positivity works from the inside out

Avoid letting your current issues, circumstances and outside pressures define you. What may be a huge obstacle now will be ancient history in five years' time. Acknowledge it, yes, address it of course, but no, don't let it define you. You define yourself by your vision, your words and, most importantly, your actions. Some leaders see themselves as victims of circumstances. When you do that you surrender control, paving the way for cynicism. Those who find joy and fulfilment in the role believe they can influence the outcome of events by their thoughts, will and actions.

As radical optimists we acknowledge [the problems] AND we look for the good there is in society as well as what we can do ourselves. Teachers are not powerless. We are the change we want to see in our schools and in society.

Rae Snape

Summary

- The root of cynicism is a sense of powerlessness.
- School leaders always have the power to make a positive difference.
- We owe it to the children and staff to be positive but, most of all, we owe it to ourselves.
- We need to analyse and challenge the basis of our cynicism in order to reduce its power and influence.
- Curiosity is a powerful antidote to creeping cynicism.
- Align yourself with positive-thinking leaders.
- Control the controllable in any given situation.
- Do not allow your current situation to define you.
- Be defined by what you stand for: your visions, words and actions.

10 Recharging the batteries

The time to relax is when you don't have time for it.

Sydney Harris

And so, we come to the last full chapter on our voyage. A chapter that I have saved until last, not because it is the least, but perhaps because it is the most important of all (and probably one of the longest). When you look out to sea, some waves you can see coming (like some parents' responses to the letter you sent out on school uniform, for example). Others seem to come right out of nowhere. Where the sea was clear a moment ago, a large and angry-looking wave is now looming large. It is wearing at times and our ability to respond effectively often depends on our mental state and how much we have left in our reserves.

For the very most part, I really enjoyed my time as a school leader (23 years must be worth a gold Blue Peter badge, surely?). But it certainly took it out of me at times. They talk about a sprint to the finish line but the approach to the finish line of the start of each school holiday felt more like a slow crawl with me on my hands and knees, desperately scrabbling on the dirt beneath me in order to pull myself over the line. When I did cross the line, I would invariably catch a cold (man flu like no other!) or get a bad back.

Sound familiar? School leadership can be highly rewarding, but there is no doubt about it: it can be demanding and stressful and can sap the energy out of you.

> As you will by now have gathered, I have a lovely new iPhone® 10 (complete with that bloody facial recognition software!). The 11 is out now but I can't afford that. I do like iPhones but I do not tend to keep up with the latest models. I only upgraded because of the battery life on my previous iPhone® 7. It does seem to me that all mobile phones are provided with a built-in obsolescence, making sure that you replace them every two to three years. The battery on my 7 was a little like my memory: not quite what it was. I needed to recharge it twice a day. If I failed to do this, the screen got really dim and if I couldn't recharge it at all, for example on long train journeys where I had not found a window seat with access to a socket, it eventually gave up altogether.

School leadership is somewhat like this, I feel. The constant demand for improved standards requires you to be a visionary, a role model, confident yet humble and accessible to all. All things to all people, in fact, and that can be very draining. If our battery is fully charged, we can generally pull this off with a good deal of strong will, bravado and positive thinking (and sometimes purely by bluffing it with the strength of our convictions), but when our batteries are depleted this becomes much more of a feat. Exhausted leaders are often more indecisive or make poor choices, and the low levels of energy tend to be picked up by staff.

As I have said before, your school or department eventually becomes like you. It is very difficult to be energised as a follower if the person you are following has worn themselves into the ground.

I have seen teachers grind themselves into the ground through working all hours. It shows how passionate they are about the job perhaps. But is it sustainable? It is very difficult to find enjoyment and fulfilment in school leadership if you are completely 'cream-crackered'.

The changing way we work

The way we work has changed in a single generation and I don't just mean in teaching.

When I was a child, my dad was the managing director of the family firm. My father worked long hours but was always back in time to read me, the youngest of five children, a bedtime story. I do not remember him doing any work at home. About one Saturday a month, he would go into work as the place was quiet and he could catch up on paperwork, sometimes taking me with him to give my mum a bit of a break (I guess my elder siblings were a bit more independent, otherwise it would not have been much of a break at all!).

Work for him, as for many others, was something you did, well, at work. Home was for family, leisure and relaxation (well, as much as anyone with five children can relax!). We often holidayed in Woolacombe in Devon and he would spend his week in splendid isolation (well, apart from his wife, five children, mother-in-law and dog). There were no emails or text messages because they, along with personal computers and smartphones, had yet to be invented. Nobody could get hold of him except in a dire emergency by ringing the hotel where we were staying. He recharged his batteries and guess what? The business coped perfectly well in his absence. Work and home life were very clearly delineated.

Fast-forward to the present day and those distinctions are rather more blurred. I have three children in their mid to late twenties (actually, by the time this is published one will have turned 30! Ouch, not quite sure where the time went). My eldest works in the car industry but will often work from home. My middle one is a council housing officer but will work from home one day a week and my youngest is a teacher and works in the evenings and usually at least half a day at the weekend.

Work, for many of us, is no longer something we just do at work. In fairness, I think the rest of society is catching up with teaching because I think those lines for teachers have been getting more and more blurred over the last 25 years. It is very hard to go through your front door of an evening and shut out the world of work because you often bring your work home with you. If you are often working in your lounge, dining room or kitchen, your mind subconsciously builds a connection between that space and work. It is bound to. It becomes a place of work.

When I am not away speaking at events, I can usually be found at home writing or preparing for my next event. As I am plugging away on my laptop, I could probably work in any room in the house (well, perhaps not the bathroom – health and safety implications!), but I try to restrict myself to working in the small box-bedroom that I use as an office. It is, I have to admit, very untidy, with books and notepads everywhere, but when I finish working for the day, I can shut the door on work both literally and mentally. It makes it easier for me to shut off. OK, that's not going to work for everyone. My kids are all grown up and have left home, so a) I have space and b) they do not need (nor want) my attention on an hourly basis, but the principle is a sound one and why the best advice is not to do your emails in bed because it blurs the lines between the world of work and a space that you associate with rest and sleep.

So, let's move on to technology, which as many will tell you is not my forte. When I first became a head, I did not own a mobile phone, so when I was on my two-day induction training, school could not get in touch with me unless it was an emergency, by ringing the hotel. Guess what? No news was good news. They coped back at the ranch! It seems weird now *not* to own a phone, but remember Julia Roberts had to knock on Hugh Grant's door to use his landline in *Notting Hill*, and that was only 20 years ago.

Don't get me wrong: smartphones are wonderful in many ways, but they have changed the way we live our lives. When I started teaching, the only way of accessing news was by buying a newspaper or by watching the one o'clock, six o'clock or nine o'clock news on TV (ten o'clock if you were watching ITV). Nowadays, you can be force-fed the news 24/7 and my BBC News app alerts me to developing stories throughout the day, and most of it is not particularly uplifting.

I love the connectivity and being able to chat with other professionals using social media. Now, I am not a natural with it but I have improved over the years and I can't deny I get a bit of a kick when something I write on Twitter gets retweeted many times, but it is quite addictive and I find myself checking my phone more than I should do to see how many times it has been retweeted and who has commented on it. The 'ping' of a retweet actually releases dopamine, the chemical associated with reward. No wonder it is addictive and many people I have spoken to admit to checking theirs dozens of times a day. I know I do.

And then there are the emails. Now that we can receive and send these on our phones, we can receive them almost anywhere. If I receive an email on my phone, assuming that it is not spam, I have to discipline myself not to reply straight away.

I know of school leaders who are very disciplined and have a work phone and email address and a separate phone for personal calls, messages and emails, turning on the work phone only on occasion over a weekend or on holiday. Equally, I know of leaders who have the one phone and would find it quite stressful not to be able to see work messages and emails as they arrive because they would find the alternative of 'not knowing what I don't know' more stressful. I do have some sympathy with this. I was on holiday a couple of years ago on the Amalfi coast of Italy and found the 'dipping out' of the wi-fi connection where we were staying a huge frustration when trying to sort out a booking enquiry. I admire the discipline of the two-phone approach, but I am not sure whether it would work for me. Horses for courses, I guess.

Time to reflect

How has the way you manage your work emails changed in recent years?

What impact have any changes had on your home–work balance?

What impact have any changes had on your mental wellbeing?

Is there a culture of 'out of work' emails in your school, and if so, what impact is this having on staff in general?

Teachers, perhaps more so than any other profession, are in danger of becoming an ever-present workforce – if not physically but digitally and, most importantly, mentally.

Stress should not be *the* major focus of teachers who want to make a difference to the communities that they serve. The focus *should* be about being happy, healthy and having the right amount of fuel in your tank to be effective, both in work and outside.

Now, there are lots of different definitions of stress. Personally, I think it is useful to make the distinction between pressure and stress. Pressure can be very motivating. Without it we can become listless and bored. It's like the engine of your car. Don't rev it and you are not going to be going anywhere.

The rev meter scenario

FIGURE 10.1a Zero pressure

Apply some pressure and the revs go up and you actually get moving. I don't write well unless I have a deadline. (Some may say I don't write well at all!) I need the pressure. But we all have an optimum level of pressure, which is different for each one of us.

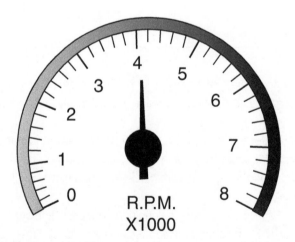

FIGURE 10.1b Optimum pressure

Go beyond that point and the needle on our rev meter starts heading over to the right-hand side of the dial. We become tired, find it hard to concentrate and start to procrastinate.

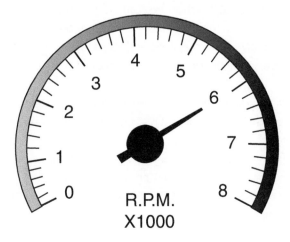

FIGURE 10.1c Mounting pressure

Push further and the car starts to object as the needle enters the danger zone.

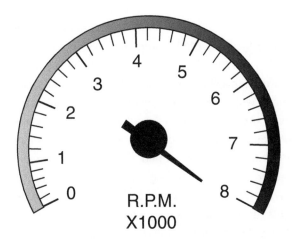

FIGURE 10.1d Excessive pressure

Stay in that danger zone for long periods and you risk damaging the engine and experiencing burnout (chronic stress). Short visits to the right-hand side of the dial are OK. This is often described as acute stress and it can be quite exhilarating. People who engage in extreme sports such as bungee jumping will often experience this, but it is short-lived and the body and mind soon have an opportunity to recover, and therein lies the most important concept: **recovery**. We can't avoid many of the pressures and stresses of modern life, but we do need to allow ourselves the opportunity to **recover** from the depletion of our reserves.

This depletion and restoration of our energy levels, our batteries, has to be an essential part of school leadership if it is to be sustainable and enjoyable.

Tal Ben-Shahar and Angus Ridgway (2017) make a very useful analogy in their book, *The Joy of Leadership*. They say that leadership is like going to the gym. Stretching your muscles and making your lungs and heart really work hard actually makes them stronger. However, working your body out too long or too hard can have the opposite effect, particularly if you do not give yourself enough time to recover between bouts of exercise.

Take the case of 1960s long-distance runner, Derek Clayton.

Struggling to make the Australian team for the 5,000- and 10,000-metre events, Clayton started to run marathons to prepare for these races. Achieving great times, Clayton made the marathons his focus, famously training longer than any of his competitors. He would run somewhere between 140 and 170 miles a week. Still six minutes shy of the world record, he drove himself to train more, often injuring himself. In 1967 he injured himself while preparing for the Fukuoka Marathon in Japan. (We hosted a wonderful teacher from Fukuoka province for six weeks once. It turned out that my pronunciation was not quite correct on first meeting. The 'u' is pronounced as an 'oo' sound, not the 'u' as in umbrella. Makes a lot of difference – very embarrassing!) Forced to take a month off training, Clayton was left with just a week before the race. He decided to take things easy and just see Fukuoka as a warm-up for his next race. Clayton broke the world record that day, becoming the first person to run a marathon in under two hours and ten minutes, shaving a full two minutes off the previous record.

Sadly, Clayton learned little from the experience and continued with the same punishing training schedule, and after seven operations on different parts of his legs he was forced to retire at the age of 32.

Unfortunately, I didn't heed my injuries, I challenged them.
Derek Clayton (quoted in Ben-Shahar and Ridgway, 2017)

Time to reflect

Being totally honest, do you…

- heed what your body and mind are trying to tell you?

- give yourself the time and space to recuperate?

Now I would show an injury the respect it deserves. I would rest it, exercise, and if need be, stop running until it healed.
Derek Clayton (quoted in Ben-Shahar and Ridgway, 2017)

School leadership is a privilege and can be very rewarding, but it is also full-on and physically and mentally demanding. You do need to build in time to recharge those depleted energy reserves or you risk burnout.

Ever wonder why you often get sick at the start of the holiday? Well, if you do not give yourself space to recharge your mind during the term, your mind stays at a high state of threat alert for extended periods, requiring the immune system to run on full throttle. As soon as you stop, your immune system drops right down, because the perceived threat level has fallen as you are at home or away on a break. You are safe. With a much-lowered immune system, you become susceptible to all sorts of ailments.

Depleting batteries

I have known **Lisa Lea-Weston** for about two years now. She is a trained therapist and founder of Talking Heads, a supervision service for senior leaders, based in Devon but operating around the UK (physically and by Skype). Supervision is an emerging profession and works on the basis of long-term relationships. Forget the image of a 1970s factory supervisor breathing down your neck and cracking the whip. It has nothing to do with that. In a school-based context, it is about getting the best possible outcomes for pupils by supporting the adults who lead the school, allowing them to offload their worries and reflect holistically on their practice without judgement. There is no reporting back: it is totally confidential to supervisor and supervisee. The most important part to me is the ability to offload, as excess baggage really depletes your batteries at an alarming rate. Had such a thing been available to me back in 2006–2007, I may well not have had six months off work! Who, as a leader, can you truly open up to? The options are pretty limited.

We were talking on the phone the other week about this issue of replenishing your reserves as a leader and Lisa said that in her experience of one-to-ones (physically or by Skype), different people need different things. As we have seen throughout this book, some people need to retreat at the weekends and holidays, but is that always enough? Crawling to the finishing line of each holiday, knowing that you can then relax, as I used to do, is somewhat flawed as a plan because:

1   Something bad might happen on the last day, e.g. a letter of complaint or some such issue that cannot be resolved until school recommences. This can be a hanging black cloud over the holiday, sapping mental reserves even further because you feel powerless.

2   You're likely to get ill on the first day of the holiday!

I know Lisa has concerns too about school leaders who survive by trying to get through to the next weekend or holiday in order to replenish their energy reserves. She encourages leaders to take five to ten minutes a day to be mindful, to do something creative and to exercise, as well as doing something in the week that fully absorbs them.

So, the big question is this: are you just surviving to get through to the next weekend or holiday, and what are you doing to replenish yourself during the working week?

Give your mind regular opportunities to recharge, preferably at least once in the middle of the week. Go into school early once a week *but* leave early and let people know that's what you are doing (it is modelling wellbeing and gives them permission to do the same). Do something for yourself. Family time, pub, cinema, evening class – something that will stop you thinking about work. **Incessant mental activity leads to burnout.**

My Twitter responders made these suggestions to help with regular recharging:

- Find time to switch off every day. It's easier during the holidays but we must find time not to do or think school each day. That could be meditation, music, prayer, sport, reading or whatever. We know we function better when we have that little break each day, whenever it comes.
- Go for a walk for five to ten minutes every lunchtime.
- It is so important that 'switching off' isn't just reserved for holidays. I've found that having hobbies separate from work is incredibly helpful in maintaining a sense of equilibrium.
- Have a hobby, whatever that might be. Walk, bake, paint, support a team, it does not really matter, but have something in your life that distracts you from work.

So, how do some of my interviewees, all resilient leaders, manage to switch off?

Jonny Mitchell says that he can switch off well in the evenings but needs routine:

- Leave work at 6 pm.
- Monday night – pub quiz.
- Wednesday night – visit parents.
- Friday night – leave work at 5 pm, meet for drink, then home.
- Weekends – taxi service to his kids.

Interestingly, Jonny says he finds switching off in the holidays harder. The first week of the summer break, he will barely give work a thought, apart from answering a few emails. Thereafter, he feels the need to do at least a couple of hours' work a week to keep mentally ticking over. He deals with the stress by being organised and keeping a holiday task list in his diary.

Hannah Wilson needs regular getaways in order to relax. Starting up two schools in two years in different age phases can be very consuming. Physically getting away helps to recharge the batteries. Going abroad with added distance helps, as does a respite from the 24/7 world of social media. A sort of digital detox.

Patrick Ottley-O'Connor describes himself as a wellbeing supermodel. You have to model work–life balance and pay as much attention to planning your life outside of school as you do your life within it. Planning trips within the UK and adventures abroad, Patrick makes sure that staff know what he has planned for his leisure time. He also thinks that it is important for them to see you leave earlier some days and arrive later at times too.

Rae Snape points out that high purpose and being a perfectionist is a potentially toxic combination. She gives a huge shout-out to the #teacher5aday movement founded by Martyn Reah, as well as the work of fellow Bloomsbury author and co-founder of Healthy Toolkit (@HealthyToolkit) Andrew Cowley. For Rae, it is no longer a binary relationship of 'work' and 'not work'. It's about things like walking the dog and looking at the sunshine, taking notice of things and being grateful. Rae suggests taking up something creative, pottery for example.

School holidays

At the start of the last summer half term in England, just as people were heading off for their break, I hit upon the genius idea of asking my teacher followers on Twitter what their top tips for switching off would be. Two things I learned very quickly:

1   Not everyone in the UK gets a summer half term, as my followers in Scotland and Northern Ireland were quick to point out! (Oops, sorry folks; didn't mean to rub it in!)

2   Twitter really is a rich source of ideas and wisdom (as well as the troll-like stuff that really shows some people in a bad light). I had so many responses and, despite my faux pas, some great suggestions even from those who were not having a half term at all.

Recognising that I do not have all the answers, I thought that I would try to group their answers into **general advice**, advice about **scheduling work** so that it does not take over your holiday, and advice on the use of **technology** (again, so that it does not take over).

Top tips for switching off in the school holidays

General advice:

• Holidays are a great time to relax, recharge, renew energy levels and rebalance your equilibrium. Do what you like to do. Love what you love to do. Aspire and plan your hopes and dreams for the future.

- Teachers need to switch off from school to get some new experiences of life that they can bring back into the classroom to inspire children. Being a role model comes with responsibilities!
- Get some pets! Nothing changes your focus like throwing the ball for a crazy pup and walking them round a field or chilling with a cat!
- Plan your holiday with the same importance you plan your term time to ensure you get a proper break. Time with people, time alone and enjoying the things you love best.
- Read for pleasure! Get lost in a good book and escape for a while. We drum it into our students, but how many of us make time to practise as we preach (or at least as much as we would like to)?
- Running.
- Yoga!
- Singing is a great way to relax. Join a choir.
- Gardening. Even if it's just growing something in pots. It's good for the soul.
- Give the people in your life who matter the most the same time, commitment and enthusiasm you give to your work on a daily basis. Heavy workloads don't just impact on you. Support those who support you.
- Writing. It can be very good for health and wellbeing.

Scheduling work:
- Switch off. Protect time for yourself. You may have to do work in the holidays but always schedule it carefully so most of the break can be work-free. Having a small section of the break where you work allows you to give yourself permission to forget about it for a significant amount of time.
- Make a plan for your time off so that you make the most of it. Put aside a specific time to complete any work that has to be done and don't work outside of that.
- Love, laugh, move, read and reflect.

Technology:
- Turn off emails and if possible don't reply to staff emails over the break. If it is urgent, they can call. Lead by example and hopefully they will do the same. Then focus on family and friends… wine helps too!
- Use work email and apps like Class Dojo on a work phone, not a personal phone.

- Leave your work phone at home, switched off, when you go on holiday.
- Create (and stick to) a staff out-of-hours email policy, for example no emails that ask for a response at the weekends or during holidays. Set clear parameters for your sanity and the wellbeing of others.
- Set time for non-work stuff. Again, stick to it.
- Change the settings on your school email address to 'out of office'. A small thing but a positive move.
- Turn off notifications on your phone.
- Stop work emails from coming through on your phone entirely.

My thanks to:
@teacher5aday, @lenabellina, @RaeSnape, @ottleyoconnor, @andrew_cowley23, @TalkingHeadsOak, @shoey1968, @jnussen, @carpool4school1, @Elspeth1972, @FarnhillMusic, @SusanMarsh50, @DKemp_01, @frankierob1, @VerityVerily, @FeDuncs, @RuthieMcC19, @formbyyoga, @JoannaCummins7, @SteveDaniels, @lemracrose, @thinkingacademy, @ChristineCouser, @si_h1972, @Mickheidie, @ygone, @AubrinS and apologies to anyone I have missed!

So, we are acknowledging that recharging the batteries is so important for school leaders, not only in the school holidays but during the working week too. What works for you?

Time to reflect

What are the biggest drains on your energy reserves? Is it working late into the evening? Too many meetings? Paperwork? Missing meals?

What helps to recharge your batteries other than taking a long holiday?

> How does it make you feel?
>
>
> Without making major lifestyle changes, how could you build more of this into your weekly routine?

Now, I have dabbled in mindfulness and am aware of its benefits. I also appreciate the positive effects that physical exercise can have on both body and mind. These days I mildly combine the two. Most days, if I am not away speaking, I manage to get to take Eddie, my golden retriever, for a good hour's walk in some fields. It is not quite as peaceful as it was a few years back, as a nearby farm has been sold off for a housing development and you can often hear the distant beep-beep of construction vehicles reversing. But for the most part, it is restful. The dog gets his exercise (although he hates getting in the car; he always has the hang-dog look of expecting to be taken to the vets, but he loves it when he runs through the fields), I get exercise, I take in my surroundings and I get to think. I am lucky, I know, but it has not always been that way.

Laughter

I think my mental wellbeing has always been linked with my ability to laugh. When I was a deputy head and throughout my first and into my second headship, I laughed a lot. I was always up for dressing-up days, back-to-front days, being the victim of a custard pie vote, water-fights and such like for Comic Relief. I played many childish pranks on people and was on the receiving end of many too (including having a brick thrown at me by a teaching assistant, only to find it was made of rubber). I took my job seriously but myself less so and I think colleagues appreciated that.

I laughed a lot outside of work at that time too, being absorbed one night a week in amateur dramatics – mostly bedroom farces with much hiding in closets – and when, in one play, staff found out that I had to strip from a Lycra® Superman outfit down to just my boxers and socks, there was a packed auditorium. Perhaps a little demeaning, looking back, but we did laugh so much in both rehearsals and performance! Parents too, some of whom got wind, also seemed to appreciate the fact that I was willing to have the p**s taken out of me. Not one person, staff or parent, ever used that against me. The ability to laugh at yourself makes you human and people respect school leaders who are human.

My breakdown in 2006–2007, in hindsight, was partly brought about by losing the ability to laugh. I started to take myself and my school's situation (particularly in relation to budget difficulties and some really challenging behaviour of pupils) so seriously that I lost sight of the fun element of work. I stopped going to amateur dramatics too, telling myself I was too busy and depriving myself of that mid-week energy boost.

So why is laughter so important?

Firstly, it allows us to avoid seeing life as permanently at high stakes and seeing everything as at risk. I recently filmed three short interviews for Carpool4School (@carpool4school1), a format taking its inspiration from Carpool Karaoke, with the wonderful Tim Barker (SENDCo) and Matt Walker (Assistant Head) from Chellaston Academy. They car share as they travel to school, much as my former deputy and I once did. Basically, you sit in the back of their car while they interview you about the book you have written and they have read, in this case *Ten Traits of Resilience*. When they arrived to pick me up, the in-car camera was already filming. I had several attempts at pulling the handle of the back door before they pointed out that it *slid* open. Not the best start to an interview but I was able to laugh at myself looking a bit of a pr*t. You can still find the video on YouTube: www.youtube.com/watch?v=SPw0Yapo6TM.

Secondly, the ability to laugh at yourself or a particular situation requires a little bit of objectivity. Objectivity allows you to take a step back, granting clarity and recognising the absurd in the otherwise threatening.

I had a parent in my first headship who was an absolute thorn in my side. Mercurial would be putting it mildly. Some days he would be helpful, for example donating a Christmas tree or items to the summer fair. But on other days he would deliver via his poor kids a three- or four-page letter of complaint (which he had clearly been up all night writing) on subjects as diverse as school dinners, head lice, the PTA and school reports. When things took a turn for the more sinister and he started sending in gifts like an angled mirror to check under our cars for incendiary devices, I contacted the police. They said they were unable to do anything because he had not made an explicit threat. Getting heartily sick of it all, one evening Richard, my deputy, and I accepted an invitation for a home visit and a tour of his sizeable grounds in a make-or-break move. It was the most bizarre evening of my life, having been shown two dresses that he claimed had belonged to a princess, whom he was not allowed to name but who had died in a tunnel, and a tour of the grounds that revealed two recently dug coffin-shaped holes. Now I have told this tale before, so forgive me, but the important point that I have not mentioned is that when we did finally escape, we cried with laughter all the way home. It was a release. A release from the tension and the knots in the stomach we had been experiencing all day.

Laughter is also a symptom of safety. **Lisa Lea-Weston** reminded me of this. Humour is vital in school leadership. It is a symptom and sign of safety and we all need to feel safe in order to thrive. It allows an emotional release that is far more positive than the alternative release of tears. You cannot laugh unless you are with someone you trust, and trust is so important.

I first met **Ritesh Patel** at #TeachmeetEnfield in 2018. He was the organiser and, as we had been talking to one another on Twitter for some time, he was kind enough to invite me along to speak. He is currently Director of Learning: Design Technology and Art at The Leigh UTC. As Ritesh pointed out in conversation for this book, we have to be realistic and accept that not everyone is blessed with a natural sense of humour, so is it important in leadership? Ritesh says, 'Ultimately, I believe so. You have to consider the context and have clear understanding, respect and emotional intelligence in your team. In my experience, it does help when faced with challenging conversations. In essence, it puts others at ease and even builds trust. This can then equate with being more approachable by colleagues and elevate a more positive presence.'

Five tips for laughter

1 Find time to re-watch TV programmes that have made you laugh out loud, particularly on a Sunday. For me in the past it has been re-runs of *Fawlty Towers*, *Dad's Army* and *Friends*, but currently *Would I Lie to You?* on Dave. Even if I am in a bad mood, the repartee between David Mitchell, Lee Mack and Rob Brydon can make me laugh out loud.

2 Within reason of course, share some of your more embarrassing moments with staff. They will appreciate your humanity and be more inclined to share theirs, dissipating tense atmospheres.

3 Choose who you sit with at meetings. I learned to avoid sitting with the serial moaners at heads' meetings because they sapped the energy right out of me. I chose to sit next to leaders who had a quirky sense of humour and could see the ridiculousness of what was often being asked of us by others.

4   Go and spend time with the kids. In their innocence they come out with such funny comments that keep us grounded.

5   Don't just wait for Comic Relief, Children in Need or World Book Day. Get out there once in a while doing something daft. Our PTA organised an 'It's a Knockout' fundraising competition (kind of a team game of *Ninja Warrior* on giant inflatables). We had a staff team and I still have a DVD, which I replay from time to time. It was such fun at a time when the school was in a financial crisis.

Sleep

The ability to get a good night's sleep is in many ways the ultimate switch-off. In the times when things in school were challenging, I would often have difficulty getting off to sleep, or if I did, I would often wake in the early hours thinking about what needed facing in the morning. I would then drift in and out of a restless sleep, only getting back off an hour before the alarm was due to go off, feeling somewhat cheated, less than equipped to cope with the business of the day and more than a little snappy. Lack of sleep would bring out the worst in me and often lead me to being indecisive on the one hand or making snap decisions on the other, some of which would then come back to bite me. Looking back on an unsatisfactory day would be likely to keep me awake the following night.

Does this sound familiar? It becomes a vicious circle and undermines our enjoyment of the job. Around 70 per cent of people in the UK report getting less than the recommended seven to eight hours' sleep a night (more in teenagers, less in older people).

So, what can we practically do to increase our chance of having a good night's kip and arriving at school the next morning feeling refreshed?

Top tips for a good night's sleep

- Avoid checking emails and using your tablet or laptop for at least an hour before going to bed.
- Try avoiding caffeine in the afternoon and evening to see if this has an impact for you.
- Drinking alcohol close to bedtime can help you to fall asleep quickly but can lead to periods of wakefulness in the night.

- Whilst exercise is good, avoid exercising close to bedtime.
- Milk contains natural sedatives, so hot, milky drinks not only return us to childhood but they calm us too.
- Try having a bowl of cereal before bedtime.
- Try herbal teabags with valarium, which is a natural sedative.
- A hot bath, or even a shower, helps to relax tight muscles brought on by the stresses of the day.
- Essential oils added to your bath or spotted onto a pillow, handkerchief or cloth can make a surprising difference to your ability to sleep. Try lavender, camomile or marjoram.
- Keep a notepad and pen by your bedside so that, if you do wake, you can commit thoughts to paper without having to hold them in your mind.
- Sounds of ocean waves are very calming and mimic breathing patterns when calm. Play these, if only through earphones, at bedtime or if you wake at night. Try the CD 'Ocean Waves at Sunset – Relax With Nature – Natural Sounds 2007' or there are a number of great free apps. Try 'Relax Melodies' by Ipnos Soft.
- Rather than counting sheep, try counting backwards slowly from 500 in time with your breathing. Counter-intuitively, it works.
- Try, when you are struggling to sleep, progressive relaxation. Start imagining your toes relaxed and work up.
- Lots of people wake in the night. If you have an alarm clock, particularly a digital one that glows the time, keep it covered, to avoid the 'it's not worth going back to sleep' syndrome.
- If you do wake, don't ruminate. Keep your mind occupied by plugging in your earphones and listening to the radio or some music. BBC Radio iPlayer is a great distraction, particularly the comedy shows.
- Keep to a regular routine of bedtimes and wake times.
- When you can't sleep or you wake up in the night, don't make going back to sleep your goal. It puts pressure on you. Rather, make your goal to relax and you will often find that sleep follows.

Leadership and self-care

My experience over the last six years of speaking and writing has been that there are many leaders out there who are fantastic at taking care of their students and staff and selfless in their service of their communities. What some of them are not so good at, however, is taking care of themselves. Perhaps they feel that they don't have the time, or that self-care is somehow, well, selfish? It could not be further from the truth. It is a little bit like gardening (I do like a metaphor as you have probably realised by now – and an exclamation mark!). I am not a born gardener; tulips, daffodils and roses are about the sum of my horticultural knowledge. However, I do know that, while I find it a bit of a chore sometimes, I need to put the effort in to maintain a healthy garden environment. Ignore the garden and it soon becomes full of weeds that choke and kill off the plants, and then it is a long way back.

Practising self-care and being compassionate to yourself as a leader is crucial not only to riding the waves but also to finding joy and fulfilment in school leadership.

Summary

- The way we work has changed, blurring traditional lines between work and home.
- Technology means that we are increasingly connected to one another as well as the world of work, making it harder to switch off.
- Teachers are in danger of becoming an ever-present workforce.
- It is useful to distinguish between pressure and stress. Pressure can be a good thing.
- Acute stress is short term. Chronic stress is a long-term condition.
- It is OK to visit the 'danger zone' for short periods **but** we need to recover afterwards.
- Start work early and finish early one day a week and do something for you that will allow your brain a break from work.
- The ability to laugh at yourself or your situation is healthy because it requires objectivity and is a symptom of safety.
- A healthy amount of sleep is essential for any leader's wellbeing, so practise good sleep hygiene.
- Self-care is not selfish but crucial to your ability to face the day and enjoy your job.

Conclusion: Mooring up

Don't work to survive. Work to create something that survives you.
Alexander den Heijer (2018)

I was reminded at the end of a recent naval documentary on the BBC that it is natural, as one comes to the end of any voyage, for a leader to look back over it and reflect. The same is true in education, whether we are finishing the school term or year, moving on to another position or retiring from the profession altogether.

There is a need to understand the impact that the voyage has had on ourselves, but also, more importantly, the impact that our leadership has had on the voyage. We want to know that our good intentions and hard labour have borne fruit, otherwise what has it all been for?

We want to know that we have left something meaningful behind us: some kind of legacy.

I am reminded of something a director of education told me years ago, which was that our contribution as a leader was like hands in a bucket of water. Remove your hands and the gulf is immediately filled. Up to a point he was correct. If we should fall under a bus tomorrow, then we should have built the leadership capacity within those we led to carry on.

Legacy is not some kind of vanity project given away at the end of a career, such as a financial bequest or a library named after us (although these may well have their places based on merit) – I, like many, spent many years in headship (far too many, in fact) battling for staff to have the buildings, support and resources to deliver great outcomes for our children and I can point to many classrooms and teaching facilities that were borne out of those labours. But nevertheless, it is more than this. It is the long-lasting impact of your time in post, beyond what you can see.

It boils down to the fact that school leaders can only leave behind three kinds of legacy:

1 **Inconsequential:** There are those leaders who are somewhat 'vanilla'. They play things safe, rarely leaving the safety of the harbour unless circumstances dictate it, or they dither and, as such, achieve little that lasts. People will come to their leaving party out of politeness but, two years down the line, you will not hear their name mentioned by students or by staff. Their time in charge was a limbo land between one phase of history and another.

2 **Negative:** Then there are those leaders who will be remembered for all the *wrong* reasons. They will leave port, sometimes putting the boat on a perilous course, perhaps for their own advancement, then jump ship. Long after they have gone, people will recall the favouritism, the public dressing downs, the harsh words unfairly said, the way they micromanaged people and used manipulation to achieve their desired outcomes. They will be remembered for their sarcasm, the broken promises and, perhaps worst of all, the times they threw staff under the bus to save their own reputation. People are very slow to forget leaders like this, if indeed they ever do. The hurt remains.

3 **Positive:** And then there are the leaders who leave behind them a positive legacy. The ones who pupils and staff talk about fondly, long after the leader has left the school or the students and members of staff themselves have.

What do these leaders have in common? They are not remembered for having the best test or exam results in the region, nor are they remembered for the shiny new schools or classrooms of chrome and glass that they have built. They are remembered for how they made other people feel.

When we move on, staff and pupils will not remember us for things we did for ourselves; rather, they will remember us for the things we did for them. The person they turned to, who offered them guidance and support; the person who picked them up when they stumbled and fell. The leader who believed in them, even when they did not believe in themselves. The leader who grew and developed the next generation of leaders.

They will not be remembered as the person who always got it right but the person who dared to leave the safety of the harbour and, despite the many challenges of the voyage, actually enjoyed riding the waves.

I am always concerned, worried I guess, that when I write about school leadership I don't spend enough time talking about the children. After all, and at the end of the day, they will be our biggest fans or critics. Rightly so. I have revisited St John's CE Primary School in Ripley, Derbyshire many times. I spent eight years there as a deputy and five as a head – half of my career. It holds a very special place in my heart. I recently set the Year 6 pupils a challenge, to write a poem about leadership from their perspective. They came up with such insightful work that I had to give them all a book voucher. Here, though, is my winning entry.

Riding the Waves

Challenges are what gives life a boost.
How you wish to face them is up to you,
At first, we are unsure how to face them.
Losing is learning, from all our mistakes.
Like riding the waves, you don't do it on your first try.
Encourage yourself to face them and not to run away.
Now you should know how to ride the waves.
Get yourself going, that is the key.
Express your knowledge to others, see if they can learn.
So, are you ready now? Ready to ride the waves?

By Albie James Sutton, Year 6 pupil at St John's CE Primary School,
   Ripley, Derbyshire

Twenty years from now, you will be more disappointed by the things you didn't do than those you did. So, throw off the bowlines. Sail away from safe harbour. Catch the wind in your sails. Explore. Dream. Discover.

Mark Twain

Postscript

A couple of years ago now, as I was finishing off my previous book, *Ten Traits of Resilience,* I was contemplating my two headships, the constant fights for funding and resources, and the numerous new classrooms and other facilities that we had managed to build against the odds. I must confess, I felt a little glow of pride, and then later that evening something rather special happened. I was at Derby Theatre (yes, Derby really does have a theatre!) hosting a local awards ceremony. During the interval a man in his thirties, tall and with thinning hair, came up to me in the bar.

'Mr Hilton?' he asked.

'Yes,' I replied rather tentatively.

'Do you remember me?' Now that he mentioned it, he did look somewhat familiar, but I could not put my finger on it. A former pupil, I was hazarding a guess.

'You really do look familiar,' I said, 'but you are going to have to help me out.'

'I am David Walker,' he said. 'You used to teach me in my final year at primary school. It was when you were a deputy head. I had only been at the school a few months and was struggling to fit in and then you cast me as Abanazar, the villain in the leavers' production of *Aladdin*. I had never been on stage before.'

'I do remember you, David, and I remember the show. You stole every scene you were in! What are you doing with yourself now?' I asked.

'I am a theatre director in Birmingham,' he replied.

I had goosebumps. I would not dream of taking credit for David's success but if I, in some small way, played a part, then that is something really special. It reminded me that our legacy as leaders is not in bricks or material things; it is in the lives we touch.

I have spent six years now writing and speaking about school leadership and wellbeing. It is not a course I planned, but one that evolved over time in an effort to help others.

Thank you for reading. I hope that in some small way, my work will continue to touch lives in the years to come.

I may not have gone where I intended to go, but I think I have ended up where I needed to be.

Douglas Adams (1989)

Oh, and one last thing… I did, eventually, learn to fold my arms properly!

Safe travels!

James

Bibliography

Achor, S. (2011), *The Happiness Advantage: The Seven Principles that Fuel Success and Performance at Work*. London: Virgin Books.

Adams, D. (1989), *The Long Dark Tea-Time of the Soul*. London: Pan Books.

American Federation of Teachers (2007), 'Building parent–teacher relationships', Washington, DC: American Federation of Teachers.

Anderson, R. J. and Adams, W. A. (2019), *Leadership at Scale*. London: Nicholas Brealey.

Baker, P. (2010), 'Education of a president', *The New York Times Magazine*, www.nytimes.com/2010/10/17/magazine/17obama-t.html

Bennis, W. (2009), *On Becoming a Leader* (4th edn.). New York, NY: Basic Books.

Ben-Shahar, T. and Ridgway, A. (2017), *The Joy of Leadership: How Positive Psychology Can Maximize Your Impact (and Make You Happier) in a Challenging World*. Hoboken, NJ: John Wiley & Sons.

Boston, R. (2014), *ARC Leadership*. London: LeaderSpace.

Brim, B. J. and Asplund, J. (2009), 'Driving engagement by focusing on strengths', *Business Journal*, https://news.gallup.com/businessjournal/124214/driving-engagement-focusing-strengths.aspx

Buck, A. (2016), *Leadership Matters: How Leaders at All Levels Can Create Great Schools*. Woodbridge: John Catt Educational.

Cain, S. (2012), 'The power of introverts', TED Talk, www.ted.com/talks/susan_cain_the_power_of_introverts

Cain, S. (2013), *Quiet: The Power of Introverts in a World That Can't Stop Talking*. London: Penguin.

Collins English Dictionary, 'Empowerment', www.collinsdictionary.com/dictionary/english/empowerment

Collins English Dictionary, 'Strength', www.collinsdictionary.com/dictionary/english/strength

Collins, J. (2001), *Good to Great: Why Some Companies Make the Leap… and Others Don't*. London: Random House.

Covey, S. R. (1989), *The 7 Habits of Highly Effective People*. London: Simon and Schuster.

den Heijer, A. (2018), *Nothing You Don't Already Know: Remarkable Reminders About Meaning, Purpose and Self-Realization*. Self-published.

Erasmus, C. (2018), 'Making positive connections with students is like doing a jigsaw', *TES*, www.tes.com/magazine/article/making-positive-connections-students- doing-jigsaw

Evans, R. (2010), *Seven Secrets of the Savvy School Leader: A Guide to Surviving and Thriving*. San Francisco, CA: Jossey-Bass.

Gerver, R. (2014), *Creating Tomorrow's Schools Today* (2nd edn.). London: Bloomsbury Education.

Gill, S. (2018), *Successful Difficult Conversations in School: Improve your Team's Performance, Behaviour and Attitude with Kindness and Success*. Woodbridge: John Catt Educational.

Goleman, D. (2017), *Leadership That Gets Results*. Boston, MA: Harvard Business Review Classics.

Goyder, C. (2014), *Gravitas: Communicate with Confidence, Influence and Authority*. London: Ebury Publishing.

Grant, A. M., Gino, F. and Hofmann, D. A. (2011), 'Reversing the extraverted leadership advantage: The role of employee proactivity', *Academy of Management Journal*, 54, (3), 528–550.

Hilton, J. (2015), *Leading from the Edge*. London: Bloomsbury Education.

Hilton, J. (2018), *Ten Traits of Resilience*. London: Bloomsbury Education.

Hodson, R. (2001), *Dignity at Work*. Cambridge: Cambridge University Press.

Kahnweiler, J. B. (2015), *The Genius of Opposites: How Introverts and Extroverts Achieve Extraordinary Results Together*. Oakland, CA: Berrett-Koehler Publishers.

Kahnweiler, J. B. (2018), *The Introverted Leader: Building on Your Quiet Strength* (2nd edn.). Oakland, CA: Berrett-Koehler Publishers.

Klein, N. and Epley, N. (2017), 'Less evil than you: Bounded self-righteousness in character inferences, emotional reactions, and behavioral extremes, *Personality and Social Psychology Bulletin*, 43, (8), 1202–1212.

Kouzes, J. M. and Posner, B. Z. (2017), *The Leadership Challenge* (6th edn.). Hoboken, NJ: John Wiley & Sons.

Kronos (2017), 'The employee burnout crisis', www.kronos.com/resource/download/23811

Loehr, J. and Schwartz, T. (2003), *The Power of Full Engagement*. New York, NY: The Free Press.

Maxwell, J. C. (2007), *The 21 Irrefutable Laws of Leadership: Follow Them and People Will Follow You* (revised edn.). Nashville, TN: Thomas Nelson.

Pink, D. H. (2013), *To Sell is Human: The Surprising Truth About Persuading, Convincing, and Influencing Others*. New York, NY: Riverhead Books.

Rath, T. and Conchie, B. (2008), *Strengths Based Leadership: Great Leaders, Teams, and Why People Follow*. New York, NY: Gallup Press.

Roarty, M. and Toogood, K. (2014), *The Strengths-Focused Guide to Leadership: Identify Your Talents and Get the Most From Your People*. Harlow: Pearson Education.

Rohn, J. (2012), *My Philosophy for Successful Living*. Melrose, FL: No Dream Too Big.

Seligman, M. E. (2018), *Learned Optimism: How to Change Your Mind and Your Life* (2nd edn.). Boston, MA: Nicholas Brealey Publishing.

Sutton, R. I. (2010), *Good Boss, Bad Boss: How to Be the Best... and Learn from the Worst*. London: Piatktus.

Sinek, S. (2011), *Start With Why: How Great Leaders Inspire Everyone to Take Action*. London: Penguin.

Walter, E. (2013), 'Four essentials of strength-based leadership', *Forbes Magazine*, www.forbes.com/sites/ekaterinawalter/2013/08/27/four-essentials-of-strength-based-leadership

Wikipedia, 'Empowerment', https://en.wikipedia.org/wiki/Empowerment

Index